The
Body Remembers
CASEBOOK

Advance acclaim for *The Body Remembers Casebook*

"*The Body Remembers Casebook* extends Babette Rothschild's earlier and widely read work, contributing to the growing acceptance of the central role of the body in the understanding and treatment of trauma. In particular, this second volume offers practitioners from all treatment modalities clear and specific guidelines for incorporating body-oriented insights and practices. And, most meaningfully, Rothschild illuminates the important principle of facilitating clients in finding their own way towards wholeness."

—Peter A. Levine, Ph.D.,
author of *Waking the Tiger, Healing Trauma*

"I was so pleased to read this book! Every psychotherapist working with traumatized clients will benefit from reading the specific case studies presented here. Each one offers solid, constructive ideas for working with this vulnerable, yet surprisingly resourceful, population in ways particularly suited to the individual sensibilities of each therapist and the unique needs of each client."

—Nancy J. Napier, LMFT,
author, *Getting Through the Day, Recreating Your Self,*
and *Sacred Practices for Conscious Living*

"This book offers something every trauma therapist needs: common sense, integration of a variety of therapeutic theories and techniques, and an awareness of the unique needs of the individual client. Too many therapists use a "cook book" approach, particularly with trauma, and this book is the antidote. Case examples throughout the book clarify the "how to's" of a basic decision tree: when and when not to employ various techniques, along with rationales. Rothschild makes a lucid case for appropriate timing and choice of a variety of interventions, showing the utility of an integrated approach to trauma treatment. She views the patient holistically, paying equal attention to both soma and psyche, and in helpful case studies, highlights the intricate interplay between the two in trauma. Every therapist should learn the lessons of this book."

—Kathy Steele, M.N., C.S.,
Clinical Director of Metropolitan Counseling Services in Atlanta, GA

A NORTON PROFESSIONAL BOOK

The
Body Remembers
CASEBOOK

Unifying Methods and Models
in the Treatment of Trauma
and PTSD

BABETTE ROTHSCHILD

W.W. NORTON & COMPANY
New York • London

The author welcomes correspondence from readers.
She may be reached at:
Babette Rothschild
P.O. Box 241778 • Los Angeles, California 90024
Telephone: 310 281 9646 • Fax: 310 281 9729
E-mail: babette@trauma.cc • Web site: www.trauma.cc

For information about permission to
reproduce selections from this book, write to
Permissions, W.W. Norton & Company, Inc.,
500 Fifth Avenue, New York, NY 10110

Production Manager Leeann Graham
Manufacturing by Haddon Craftsmen, Inc.

Library of Congress Cataloging-in-Publication Data

Rothschild, Babette.
The body remembers casebook : unifying methods and models in the treatment of trauma
and PTSD / Babette Rothschild.
p.   cm.
"A Norton professional book."
Includes bibliographical reference and index.
ISBN 0-393-70400-9
1. Post-traumatic stress disorder—Treatment.   2. Psychic trauma—Treatment.   3.
Psychotherapy.   I. Title.
[DNLM: 1. Stress Disorders, Post-Traumatic—therapy—Case Report. 2.
Psychophysiology—Case Report. 3. Psychotherapy—methods—Case Report. WM 170
R847ba 2003]
RC552.P67   R685   2003
616.85'21—dc21   2002038065

W. W. Norton & Company, Inc., 500 Fifth Avenue, New York, N.Y. 10110
www.wwnorton.com

W. W. Norton & Company Ltd., Castle House, 75/76 Wells St., London W1T 3QT

In the broader definition of "family" . . .

To my siblings:
Melanie, with whom I share genes,
and Jeanne, Bob, Peter, and Susan with whom I don't.
You each have a special place in my heart.

Contents

Contents

Contents

Acknowledgments

One of the great privileges of publishing a book is being able to publicly thank those who inspired and helped.

As this volume primarily comprises cases, my first thanks go to my clients, supervisees, and students, who have taught me so much and inspired the chapters herein both directly and indirectly. Without them, I would not have had any material for this book.

Next, I want to express my gratitude to the creators of the theories, methods, and models featured among these pages. Their insights and creativity have contributed much to the field of psychology and to the treatment of traumatized individuals. I would also like to thank those who taught and trained me, helping me to become competent in my craft.

I am ever indebted to my colleagues David Grill, Kathy Downing, Betta de Boer-van der Kolk, Sima Juliar Stanley, Michael Gavin, Mary

Hart, Alan Berkowitz, Vicki Salvin, and especially John May for their considered and rigorous comments on various versions of this manuscript. Their applause sustained me, but their criticism made this a better book.

This cannot go to print without also thanking Margaret Stanley and Karin Rhines for their constant support and encouragement. No one could want for more enthusiastic cheerleaders!

Finally, I would like to say how lucky I feel to have Norton as my publisher. Though I know they have plenty of authors, I never feel like a "little fish." Every member of their staff, in every department, is an enthusiastic and competent partner through each step of the publishing process. I would like to thank those whom I have dealt with personally, including: copyeditor Casey Ruble, marketing manager Kevin Olsen, foreign rights manager Elisabeth Kerr, associate managing editor Michael McGandy, credit manager Kathryn Pinto, and editorial assistant Andrea Costella in New York; and Katy Lloyd, publicist, in London.

Changing editors can be "traumatic" for many authors, and I do miss Susan Munro, my first editor, who founded Norton Professional Books in the mid-1980s. When Deborah Malmud came on board to replace her as the new director, I wondered how she would be able to fill such exceptionally competent shoes. But fill them she does, to overflowing, with tremendous skill and clarity, and a great sense of humor. Hats off to you, Deborah! Thank you for all of your help and for your part in making the writing of this book so much fun.

Introduction

The main goal of this book is to inspire psychotherapists working with traumatized individuals to learn as much as possible about theory, tools, and treatment so that they can be well-equipped in working with the unpredictability of trauma and the diverse needs of clients.

The cases presented here are not meant to provide instruction on how to do trauma therapy in a particular, or even several particular, ways. The aim is, instead, to promote the practice of learning and then applying a variety of methods in combinations tailored to the specific needs of each client.

A further goal is for therapists to learn to trust and use their own common sense as a complement to, and sometimes in lieu of, what they have been taught—to become able to recognize when interventions are not helping a client even when they "should," and when interventions that "should not" be helpful actually are.

ON COMMON SENSE

While I was living in Denmark, a window washer expressed interest in my work. When I told him what I did he asked, "What tools do you use for that?" It was an intriguing question. He wasn't asking me to give him a lecture on psychotherapeutic theory and method. His inquiry was much more basic and concrete; he was a workman and lived by his tools. I wanted to answer his question truthfully, but it was a challenge to do so. After thinking about it for a minute, I replied, "I think my biggest tool is common sense—and that is something they did not teach me at the university." He looked me straight in the eye and smiled, "Yes, we all need plenty of that in our work."

Common sense is probably the first, most important ingredient of safe trauma therapy—of making any psychotherapy safe, for that matter. However, it is astonishing to realize that common sense is rarely mentioned, let alone taught, in courses on theory or treatment. My London friend and colleague Michael Gavin can account for this omission, though: "Common sense," he likes to say, "isn't so terribly common."

There is a disturbing trend in psychotherapy, particularly in trauma therapy. Practitioners are becoming overly dependent on techniques that are learned and applied in a systematized manner, and are neglecting common sense and theory as aids to adapt these tools to the specific needs of individual clients. It is not that I find the protocols are lacking; actually, most of them are quite good. What is lacking too often, however, is thoughtful consideration before and during their application. When therapy methods are applied uniformly like a recipe, their potential for harm increases, no matter how good they are.

Merriam-Webster's Collegiate Dictionary defines common sense as "sound and prudent but often unsophisticated judgement." For the window washer this might mean discarding a recommended cleaning product that does not perform as promised, putting off washing outer windows when rain is threatening, or avoiding a shaky ladder. Examples of applying common sense to trauma therapy include: laying aside or changing a technique or protocol that makes a client worse, putting off the approach to potentially distressing material until the client feels safe, adjusting the length of therapy to the client's needs, or using basic theory to create appropriate interventions.

ELIMINATING CLIENT BLAME

In 1969 Joseph Wolpe, founder of behavior therapy, cautioned his students to look for the cause of treatment failures within the application of their therapeutic methods, *not* within their clients. He went on to warn that failures of behavior therapy should not be attributed to client "resistance" or investment in "secondary gain." Wolpe believed that successful client change was the only justification for continuing with a particular method. In its absence, he advised, something different must be tried.

Our clients would greatly benefit from a broad application of Wolpe's wisdom to all schools of psychotherapy, and particularly to today's methods of trauma therapy. We are at a particularly difficult juncture as trauma practitioners: Competition for the superiority of one method or model over another is fierce. This trend puts clients in a difficult position: Should they prioritize choosing a method or is it more important to find a practitioner who is a good fit? Too many trauma therapists offer only one technique, which leads to questions regarding client commitment when that method fails. In such circumstances, the client can be hurt.

Even the most effective medicine cannot cure all patients. Witness the miracle of penicillin, which was an incredible boon to public health in the wake of World War II. However, penicillin is not a miracle drug for the patient who is allergic to it; symptoms range from the uncomfortable to the fatal.

Of course, in terms of life or death, psychological treatment methods are less risky than penicillin. But some clients suffer unnecessary distress, become retraumatized, or even decompensate from the use of methods that are advantageous to others. Preferably, the choice of method is never perfunctory, but rather decided upon in consideration of and consultation with the client. And it is always a good idea to have other methods at hand in case the chosen method fails.

AN INSPIRING PROTOTYPE

In 1998 I witnessed a particularly poignant presentation at the annual meeting of the International Society of Traumatic Stress Studies. I had the privilege of being on the panel of the special symposium Issues in Creative and Body-Oriented Approaches to Trauma Treatment, chaired by David Read Johnson. The presentation of Betta de Boer-van der Kolk knocked my socks off. At that point in time, de Boer-van der Kolk, a clinical social worker who had not previously been exposed to body approaches, and her husband Bessel van der Kolk had been exploring applications of body psychotherapy to trauma treatment for several years. De Boer-van der Kolk had used herself, and her own trauma, to investigate the effectiveness of several methods. Those explorations became the theme of her paper "Integrating Body-Oriented Techniques in a Conventional Psychodynamically Oriented Clinical Practice." In it she described her personal experiences in resolving a serious car accident that had occurred in her youth and continued to affect her life into her early fifties. What was remarkable about her experience, and the retelling of it, was how clearly she was able to describe the relevant contributions from diverse therapies. The two methods from which she sought help clearly met different needs. The first, Al Pesso's psychomotor therapy, was instrumental in changing her feeling of isolation, helping her get back in touch with herself through repatterning the imprint of her family's response following the trauma. The second, Peter Levine's somatic experiencing, helped her body to regain pretrauma homeostasis. It was clear from her presentation that either method alone, although helpful, would have left the resolution of that past event incomplete. The two therapies were consistent and compatible complements.

De Boer-van der Kolk's powerful presentation illustrated plainly how important it is for survivors of trauma to have access to multiple therapy methods and that no one method can address all issues. But what if this is not possible? Some clients do not have access to more than one therapist for economic reasons. For others, the risks of complications of transference are a deterrent. However, there is nothing to hinder professionals from becoming trained in multiple methods in order to attend to the needs of their clients. And, when those obstacles do not exist, the road is open for therapists to cooperate with colleagues in team-treating individuals.

ORGANIZATION OF THE BOOK

This book is meant to encourage therapists to train in several treatment modalities so that treatment plans can be tailored to the needs and tastes of the client. The therapies illustrated here are not meant for replication, though some aspects may be useful and easy to learn. The case examples are presented to illustrate what is possible when different models are applied in varying combinations.

There are *many* more models available than are included in this volume. I have chosen the methods presented here because they are the ones with which I am most familiar. Absence of a particular method in no way implies negative criticism. Choosing therapy models to train in is a matter of taste and personal style. Those included in this book reflect my taste and my style. It is up to each psychotherapist to choose which ones suit his own.*

Each chapter spotlights one or more models that I have found useful in conjunction with the principles and interventions outlined in *The Body Remembers* (Rothschild, 2000). I have varied the writing style, interspersing chapters written as narratives and session-by-session descriptions with those that are primarily single-session transcripts. In general, therapy methods that are more containing (braking) are discussed before those that have the potential to be arousing (accelerating).

Many current therapies and interventions have foundations in earlier methods. I always try, albeit imperfectly, to give credit to the source of the methods and strategies discussed. I hope that readers and originators will forgive any mistakes or omissions, as none are intentional.

DISCLAIMER

It is no longer possible for me to begin a lecture, class, or book without repeating my standard disclaimer, in this case adapted to the particulars of this volume.

The book you are about to read comprises theory and speculation. Some of the therapy methods discussed herein have been formally

---

* *I have attempted to alternate the use of the pronouns he, she, him, her, his, and hers throughout the text.*

studied, some have not. The client cases described do not prove the efficacy of a given method or methods; each is anecdotal. The opinions expressed are mine unless otherwise cited.

During a recent discussion with my personal physician, I challenged her recommendation for treatment. Instead of becoming offended, she remarked, "Well, you could be right. You know, today's gospel is tomorrow's heresy, and vice versa." This wise response increased my confidence in her. Had she insisted that she was the authority, or that there was only one right way, I would have looked for a new doctor. In medicine this tenet is well-founded, as it is in science. It is also applicable to psychology. Diagnostic criteria change often—witness the evolution of the American Psychiatric Association's *Diagnostic and Statistical Manual* (DSM), now in its fourth edition. Likewise, treatment methods come into vogue and fade into the background. There is nothing we can say works for sure and certainly nothing that works for everyone.

It is my hope that this book reflects the respect I have for the diverse practices, methods, models, opinions, and preferences of my colleagues and readers.

READER SELFCARE

One of my basic tenets is that trauma therapy does not have to be traumatizing. That philosophy extends to my lectures and trainings, and also to my writing.* Though it is impossible to eliminate all risk, it is not fundamental for a book on trauma to be traumatizing to the reader.

---

* *Although many professionals have heard stories much worse than those described in the cases in this book, some readers may have had little exposure to traumatic incidents. Those who know they are emotionally vulnerable to reading material on trauma (or those who worry about that possibility) may be helped by this section. Others may prefer to skip it.*

What we have come to call *vicarious traumatization* is a risk for anyone exposed to the traumatic events of others. Vulnerability is not bounded by role. Volunteers, professionals, and even family and friends can be affected. The sequelae of trauma can be communicable in many ways, including through the media. The world over, individuals are affected by the trauma of others, through witnessing events on television, hearing reports on the radio, reading accounts in print media and books, and talking with others.

Just as survivors of trauma vary in their vulnerability to PTSD, so too do people, including psychotherapists, vary in their vulnerability to vicarious traumatization. Reading materials with descriptions of traumatic events, like those included here, pose a risk for vicarious traumatization, *depending on reader vulnerability*. Though attention has been paid to reducing risk as much as possible through careful editing, all risk cannot be eliminated.

Preventing Vicarious Trauma from Written Media

A good way to reduce the risk of falling victim to vicarious trauma while reading provocative material is to pay attention to what is happening in your body, both physically and emotionally. Body awareness is your single best gauge of how something is affecting you. When hyperarousal occurs, it can be helpful to take a calming break. There are several reasons for this. First, it is not usually desirable to become upset from reading professional material. Taking breaks will make it possible to modulate the level of arousal. The second reason for taking breaks is that as hyperarousal increases, the activity of the hippocampus (a part of the brain associated with explicit memory and contextual thinking) becomes suppressed by the hormones released. This means that the higher the level of arousal, the less one is able to think clearly and digest or even remember the material one is reading. So, at the very least, it is a waste of time to read while hyperaroused, regardless of whether it causes long-term distress.

Next, it may be helpful to learn to avoid picturing the trauma situations in your mind's eye. Creating imagery—visual, auditory, and touch-, taste-, and smell-related—of traumatic events brings them much closer to the self. The more real a situation feels to you, the more risk there will be of vicarious traumatization.

Finally, listen to your internal dialogue. What you say to yourself does matter. How are you talking to yourself about what you are reading? Try to eschew language that increases your identification with the people and traumas you are reading about. The more you can separate yourself from them, the less you will risk vicarious traumatic reactions.

The
Body Remembers
CASEBOOK

Part One

THEORY
AND
PRACTICE

∾

CHAPTER ONE

Reviewing
The Body Remembers

To best utilize this casebook, the reader should be familiar with several concepts discussed in depth in *The Body Remembers*: *The Psychophysiology of Trauma and Trauma Treatment*. To that end, this chapter summarizes the subjects that are most relevant to the cases discussed herein. For a more complete discussion of these and other topics, the reader is referred to the original book.

DEFINING POSTTRAUMATIC STRESS DISORDER (PTSD)

The diagnostic category PTSD is relatively new in the annals of psychology. It first appeared in the third edition of the DSM (APA, 1980). The definition of the condition is unusual for two reasons. First, most categories of diagnosis in the DSM are symptom-dependent; clients displaying a certain number of particular symptoms qualify for a specific diagnosis. PTSD, on the other hand, is situation-dependent. That is, there must be an identifiable event that qualifies as "traumatic" for the diagnosis of PTSD to apply. No matter the symptoms, if no event is pinpointed, the diagnosis cannot be made. Second, the original definition of PTSD depended upon majority rule, the "existence of a recognizable stressor that would evoke significant symptoms of distress *in almost everyone*" (my emphasis; p. 238). In further editions of the DSM, that benchmark was dropped in favor of a standard that is broader and more reasonable.

As of this writing, the latest edition of the DSM (APA, 1994) recognizes that PTSD can result from exposure to events that are or are perceived as threatening to one's own life or limb, witnessing violence to or the violent death of another, or learning about violence to or the violent death of a relative or close associate. Further, this definition recognizes that children may suffer PTSD from "developmentally inappropriate sexual experiences without threatened or actual violence or [physical] injury" (p. 424). In addition to experiencing a precipitating event, an individual qualifying for the diagnosis of PTSD must have a symptom profile that includes a reexperiencing of the causal event (often, but not always, in the form of intrusive images), avoidance of reminders of the event, and persistent symptoms of hyperarousal (sleep disturbance, concentration difficulties, hypervigilence, etc.; APA, 1994).

Distinguishing Stress, Traumatic Stress, PTS, and PTSD

The core of PTSD is *stress*, a condition identified by Hans Selye (1956). Stress results from any demand on the body, including demands of a positive nature such as acrobic exercise, competing on a TV game show, or having sex.

The most extreme stress is *traumatic stress*, which is a predictable consequence of exposure to traumatic incidents. It is traumatic stress that causes hyperarousal in the body's nervous system, making it possible to fight, flee, or freeze in response to threat. As a result, normal homeostasis is disturbed for a period of time. It is usual for symptoms to heighten and then gradually diminish over a period of hours, days, or even weeks. For example, after the events of September 11, 2001, many people around the world suffered from the hyperarousal of traumatic stress: nervousness, sleep disturbance, nightmares, changes in appetite, difficulty concentrating, etc. For even up to several weeks, these responses can be considered normal. But if symptoms prevent adequate functioning, a diagnosis of *acute stress disorder*—a short-term version of PTSD—may apply. What is not normal, however, is when symptoms of traumatic stress persist months or years after an event is over (hence the prefix "post").

When that happens, the term *post*traumatic stress (PTS) applies. PTS is not a disorder in itself. Further symptoms and dysfunction must be present to warrant a PSTD diagnosis. Many people function quite well with PTS, or what some call "subclinical PTSD." However, it is worth paying attention to PTS, as it appears it can accumulate and grow from exposure to multiple events and can reach a degree where symptoms would then qualify as a *disorder*. This possibility may help to explain how a seemingly well-functioning individual can suddenly suffer from PTSD following what appears, on the surface, to be a minorly stressing event.

The clinical pictures of traumatic stress and PTS, or acute stress disorder and PTSD, may be indistinguishable. Those with traumatic stress from a recent event or PTS from a distant one may voice similar complaints while they continue to function in their daily lives. Likewise, someone suffering from acute stress disorder and someone with PTSD may exhibit the same symptoms and level of dysfunction. The determining factor within either of these pairings is the proximity of the precipitating traumatic event. However, the treatment of choice may differ greatly depending on when the event occurred. The client suffering from a recent traumatic event will probably have different clinical needs than someone whose symptoms have been long-standing.

SOMATIC CONSEQUENCES OF TRAUMA

Although emotional response to any life event affects the body, trauma does so to the utmost. During a traumatic incident the neurotransmitters released from the brain's limbic system signal an alarm to the autonomic nervous system (ANS). These hormones activate one of the branches, the sympathetic nervous system (SNS), to its most extreme arousal: preparation for fight and/or flight. Blood flows away from the skin and viscera and into the muscles for quick movement. Heartrate, respiration, and blood pressure all rise to give the muscles more oxygen. The eyes dilate to provide sharper distant sight. All of these elements of SNS arousal are necessary to respond to threat. When fight or flight are not possible or have not been successful, the limbic system may further signal the ANS to *simultaneously* activate its other branch, the parasympathetic nervous system (PNS). The SNS continues its extreme arousal while the PNS freezes the action of the body—the muscles becoming either slack like a mouse caught by a cat or stiff like a deer caught in headlights (Gallup & Maser, 1977). What looks like paralysis or deadness to the outside observer, though, is misleading. The resulting internal strain of this extreme and simultaneous arousal is something akin to holding tight on the reins of a horse about to bolt out of control. Those who have experienced freezing commonly report that during such an episode time slows down and body sensations and emotions are numbed; it appears to be a kind of dissociation. As freezing only occurs when the individual's perception is that the threat is extreme and escape impossible, these reactions make perfect sense: People who have survived mauling by animals or falls from great heights report that this kind of dissociation reduces the physical pain and emotional terror during such experiences.

Successful fight or flight is usually enough to discharge the arousal of the SNS. Most people experiencing traumatic events do not end up in need of psychiatric intervention. However, the outcome with freezing can be quite different.

Though freezing is an excellent survival mechanism—the "dead" mouse wakes up and escapes after the cat has lost interest—it appears to exact a higher psychophysical price in the wake of a traumatic incident than the responses of fight and flight. Freezing during a traumatic event is a major predictor of who develops PTSD (Bremner et al., 1992; Classen, Koopman, & Spiegel, 1993). People who have frozen during traumatic incidents and survived appear to have greater difficulty coming to terms with their trauma. Somatic symptoms abound as the hyperarousal in both SNS and PNS persist chronically or are easily set in motion by internal or environmental triggers.

Because symptoms of anxiety and panic disorders also reflect ANS hyperarousal, it is easy to assume that they are caused by trauma. However, it is important to remember that PTS or PTSD cannot be assumed unless a causal event is identified. Still, many of the interventions and techniques used to reduce and contain hyperarousal with trauma clients are also useful with those affected by anxiety and panic.

PUTTING ON THE BRAKES

The first goal of any trauma therapy must be helping the client to contain and reduce hyperarousal. A useful metaphor for that process is *putting on the brakes*. When engaging anything that is powerful and potentially dangerous—whether it is a machine or an emotional process—knowing how to stop it is a prerequisite for safety. Like automobiles without well-functioning brakes, trauma processes can easily become overwhelming. When that is allowed to happen, retraumatization is the unfortunate result. Like a car speeding out of control with the accelerator pressed to the floor, "traumatic acceleration" is, simply, extreme, uncontrolled hyperarousal. Developing and using "trauma brakes" can prevent such out-of-control acceleration and the resulting retraumatization. Equipping a client with tools to slow down or stop traumatic acceleration will aid the therapy immensely. Clients who know they can stop or pull back from unpleasant memories have more courage to address them. Giving them control is an antidote to the out-of-control nature of traumatic events. Learning to apply the brakes is a necessary prerequisite for addressing traumatic memories. It is especially helpful for clients with whom direct work on traumatic material is either not possible or not advisable.

WHAT IS BODY MEMORY?

There are basically two major categories of memory: explicit and implicit. Explicit memory is conscious and requires language. It comprises concepts, facts, events, descriptions, and thoughts. Implicit memory, on the other hand, is unconscious. It is made up of emotions, sensations, movements, and automatic procedures. The terms "body memory" and "somatic memory" suggest the implicit.

The concept of body memory is easily misunderstood. It is not the body, per se, that holds a memory itself; the brain stores the memory. Body memory means, more precisely, an intercommunication between the brain and the body's nervous systems: autonomic, sensory, and somatic. When, for example, you remember how to ride a bicycle, it is not your muscles that actually remember the movement, though they are a crucial part of the process. The memory was laid down when you first learned to ride. At that time the sensory and somatic nerves in your leg's muscles and connective tissues communicated new patterns of movement (getting on and riding, how to balance, etc.) to your brain. It is there that those patterns were recorded and stored. Now, when it is time for you to hop on a bike, the same patterns are recalled from the brain, which sends messages back to those same tissues in your legs to replicate the same movements. Body memory is unconscious, implicit memory. It is automatic; you don't have to think about it. That is, for example, why once you learn to ride a bicycle, type, or swim, you don't (usually) have to learn it ever again. Those patterns of movement are stored forever in the brain.

There are those who argue that body memory is held in the muscles themselves, and even at a cellular level. While this could be true (though not yet proven) at least as far as movement is concerned, the memory that is stored in the brain is what is crucial. If that were not the case, those suffering from spinal injuries would still be able to move their limbs, walk, and so on. However, spinal cord injury interrupts communication between the brain and muscles resulting in paralysis—the muscles no longer receive instructions regarding how or when to contract and cause movement. In cases of limb amputation, memory of sensations and movements (phantom limb phenomena) continue to exist in the absence of the associated limb. This is because the somatic memory of the lost limb is stored in the brain.

The body also remembers traumatic events. Body sensations that constitute emotions (e.g., terror) and physical states (e.g., pain or ANS arousal) and the patterns that make up movements (e.g., fight, flight, freeze) are all recorded in the brain. Sometimes the corresponding explicit elements—e.g., the facts of the situation, a description of the events—are simultaneously recorded; sometimes they are not.

TRAUMATIC MEMORY VS. MEMORY OF OTHER EVENTS

The Amygdala and Hippocampus

Within the limbic system of the brain are two related areas that are central in memory storage: the *hippocampus* and the *amygdala*. The last few years have produced a growing body of research that indicates these two parts of the brain are essentially involved in response to, and memory of, traumatic events (Nadel & Jacobs, 1996; Post et al., 1998; van der Kolk, 1994). It is believed that the amygdala's job is to register highly charged emotions, such as terror and horror, along with the body sensations that identify them. The amygdala becomes very active when there is a traumatic threat. This is the part of the brain that signals the survival alarm that eventually leads to the ANS preparing the body for fight, flight, or freeze. Memories of terror and horror, including concomitant body sensations and protective or defensive movements, are not stored in the amygdala but must be processed through the amygdala in order to be recorded as implicit memories in the brain's cortex.

The hippocampus, on the other hand, is necessary to the eventual storage of information that helps us make cognitive sense of our memories—for example, to contextualize them in time and space. The hippocampus helps to put our memories into their proper perspective and slot in our life's timeline. As with the amygdala, memory is not stored in the hippocampus, but the information must be processed through it before being recorded as explicit memory in the cortex.

The importance of the hippocampus in traumatic memory becomes clear when one looks at what can happen to memory while recording a traumatic event. When the arousal in the ANS becomes very high, the activity of the hippocampus can be suppressed by the wealth of stress hormones released. When that happens, its usual function of lending context to a memory is not possible. The result may be that the traumatic event is prevented from becoming a "memory" in the usual sense of the word: A piece of information about oneself that lies clearly in one's past. Instead, elements of the past experience are unable to anchor in time. They seem to float freely, often invading the present. In the absence of hippocampal activity, memories of unresolved traumatic incidents may remain in the implicit memory system alone. There images, sensations, and emotions can all be provoked, but without engagement of the explicit memory system, they cannot be narrated (cohesively recounted) or understood. It is this mechanism that is behind the PTSD symptom of *flashback*—episodes of reliving the trauma as if it is happening now.

Also affecting the memory of traumatic events as mediated by the hippocampus is the ability to think clearly during the event. When stress is combined with fear or anxiety, the ability to think clearly can be compromised. A common, if trivial, example is game show contestants, who often comment that it is much easier to answer correctly when watching the show from home than it is while in the studio.

The ability to make sense of traumatic events at the time of their occurrence is often reduced because of the combination of extreme fear and stress escalated to hyperarousal. This phenomenon further supports the idea that trauma therapy is best conducted with the brakes on. Keeping the level of hyperarousal low helps ensure that the client will be able to think, integrate, and make sense of what is processed in therapy. When a client is so afraid that he is not able to make sense of what happened, or, for that matter, what is occurring at any moment in the therapy setting, it is a sure sign that somewhere in him, the stress level is too high and it is time to put on the brakes.

Dissociated Elements of Experience

Memory of any event is made up of the components of that experience. Peter Levine's (1992) SIBAM model is a useful way to conceptualize this. The model was developed in an effort to understand dissociation of memory. Levine identifies five major elements—sensations, images, behaviors, affects, and meanings—common to any experience. Usual memories of nontraumatic events hold all of these elements intact. Recall triggered by one of the elements usually elicits the others. This is a common experience: Remember the last time you were reminded of a pleasant time in your life by the smell from a bakery or a particular song. This kind of memory recall happens from time to time to nearly everyone.

Memory of traumatic events, however, can be different. Though sometimes a traumatic event is remembered in its entirety, it is more common for it to be remembered piecemeal and dissociated. That is, some of the elements appear to be missing while others are highlighted. One client might have visual flashbacks of an event, indicating that she remembers images and has emotional reactions to them (terror), but lacks awareness of body sensations and the narrative (meaning) that can make sense of the flashbacks. A child might reenact his trauma during play, indicating that behaviors are remembered, but have no recall in images or of facts that could tell where or why his behaviors originated.

The most troublesome traumatic memories are those that involve body sensations and little else. In such cases, the body sensations associated to the traumatic memory are intact, but the other elements, particularly the cognitive aspects—i.e., facts, narrative, time and space context (mediated by the hippocampus)—that could help the individual to make sense of the memories appear lost. Working with implicit, trauma-based sensations in the absence of a trauma narrative can be difficult. The explicit memory may or may not emerge. In such cases it is sometimes necessary to find ways to ease the symptoms and/or increase their containment, as their origin might never be known. At the same time, reducing hyperarousal as a goal in itself sometimes makes it possible to recall an otherwise lost event.

EVALUATING CLIENTS FOR TRAUMA THERAPY

It is extremely important to remember that *not all clients benefit from work with specific traumatic memories*, and some even become worse. Distinguishing who is a candidate for therapy that is primarily containing—e.g., putting on the brakes, (re)developing resources, building life skills—and who can manage a therapy that increases hyperarousal—presses on the accelerator by addressing traumatic memories with various methods—is crucial to safe and successful trauma therapy.

A complete case history is always necessary to assess any new client. It is tempting to skip this step with those who come to work specifically on a single trauma, but that is inadvisable. Restricting attention only to information about a single event is like looking at a two-dimensional picture—there is much unknown and unseen that could land both client and therapist in trouble. A much better idea is to create a multidimensional picture of each client. It is particularly important to evaluate current and past resources, attachment issues, physical and mental health history, and drug and alcohol history and current usage. Many therapists construct genograms (McGoldrick, Gerson, & Shellenberger, 1999) or use instruments to evaluate current functioning, such as the Impact of Events Scale (Weiss, 1996), Somatoform Dissociation Questionnaire (SDQ-20) (Nijenhuis, Spinhoven, van Dyck, van der Hart, & Vanderlinden, 1996), and the Dissociative Experiences Scale (DES) (Carlson, 1996). Finding the assessment tools and methods that give you the information needed to enhance your work is a matter of clinical judgment. Those mentioned here are examples—not necessarily recommendations. Find what works best for you and the types of clients you work with.

Client Types

Lenore Terr made the first proposal for categorizing trauma clients: Her definition of Type I refers to clients who have experienced a single traumatic event; Type II are those who have been repeatedly traumatized (Terr, 1994). Though a good beginning, it is helpful to further break down Type II clients into subgroups:

Type IIA clients are those who have experienced multiple traumas but are able to separate the individual traumatic events from each other. This type of client can speak about a single trauma at a time and can, therefore, address one at a time. Usually these clients have an early history that includes stability and healthy attachment. Thus, they have many resources, including resilience.

Type IIB individuals are so overwhelmed with multiple traumas that they are unable to separate one traumatic event from the others. Type IIB clients begin talking about one trauma but quickly find links to others. The stress level is so high that making sense of any or all of the events becomes impossible—they appear (and may be) linked and interconnected.

Type IIB(R) clients have a stable background, but the complexity of traumatic experiences is so overwhelming that they can no longer maintain resilience.

Type IIB(nR) clients have an unstable background bereft of resources for resilience. Features of borderline personality disorder are often seen in these clients. Those with dissociative identity disorder represent the extreme of this type.

Evaluating a trauma client's type can help give clues to therapeutic direction and choice of method. For example, Type I and Type IIA individuals usually require less attention to the therapeutic relationship and have less tendency to develop an intense transference to the therapist. They can often move quickly to working directly with the traumatic incident(s) that brought them to therapy.

For Type IIB clients, on the other hand, resource (re)building through the therapeutic relationship is a prerequisite to addressing traumatic memories directly. For those with stable, resource rich, backgrounds, reacquainting resources is in order. But with clients who have had little opportunity for resource-building, it is necessary to build many resources from scratch. For the Type IIB(nR) client, working on the therapeutic relationship is the most important, constituting a significant part, if not all, of the therapy.

Integration and resolution of traumatic experiences in both mind and body is the goal of trauma therapy. To accomplish that, all of the above principles need to be gathered and applied as treatment interventions regardless of the methods used. Integrated trauma therapy is the topic of the next chapter.

CHAPTER TWO

Integrated Trauma Therapy:

PRINCIPLES, METHODS,
AND MODELS

Nearly every model of psychotherapy, body psychotherapy, and trauma therapy will be helpful if applied to the appropriate client at the proper time, with common sense, patience, and attention to client feedback. Our clients are our best experts on what works for them: If we ask the right questions, they will be able to tell us during and after each session and course of treatment what works for them and what does not. No one method is one-size-fits-all; accepting that fact—recognizing that there are always limitations when dealing with individuals who each have widely varied needs—is an example of common sense.

TEN FOUNDATIONS FOR SAFE TRAUMA THERAPY

The ten foundations of safe trauma therapy, first printed in *The Body Remembers*, form the basis for this casebook. They are included here with additional commentary:

1. *First and foremost: Establish safety for the client within and outside the therapy.*

   Judith Herman first taught us the importance of this principle in *Trauma and Recovery* (1992). Working with trauma involves helping the client loosen the defenses that have been used to cope with trauma. If the client is not living in a safe situation, or if the therapy situation does not feel safe, then a loosening of those defenses can lead to decompensation or even increase vulnerability to further harm.

2. *Develop good contact between therapist and client as a prerequisite to addressing traumatic memories or applying any techniques—even if that takes months or years.*

   Research consistently indicates that the therapeutic relationship is one of the most powerful factors affecting the outcome of psychotherapy. This also applies to trauma therapy. Without a therapeutic alliance, the client will not feel safe to address the terror of her past. Of course, there will be marked differences in how central a role the therapeutic relationship plays in individual therapy, but a solid alliance is always a necessary part.

3. *Client and therapist must be confident in applying the "brake" before they use the "accelerator."*

   As with an automobile, safe therapy requires that you know how to stop a trauma process before you set it in motion or accelerate it. Working with trauma can be uncertain and potentially volatile. You never really know how a client will react to an intervention, or, for that matter, to a simple question, the color of your shirt, or the smell of your coffee. One of the features of PTSD is that traumatic memory can be easily triggered. When that happens, hyperarousal accelerates out of control, causing intense physical symptoms and/or flashbacks. Until triggers are identified, they are unpredictable—literally anything can be a trigger. In order for clients to feel safe in life and also in therapy, they need to be equipped with tools to help them contain reactions to therapy and triggers, and to halt the out-of-control acceleration of hyperarousal. Being able to "put on the brakes" will aid clients in their daily life, as well as give them courage to address difficult issues. Once clients know where the brake is, they are in control of rather than at the mercy of, their process.

4. *Identify and build on the client's internal and external resources.*

In general, resources mediate the negative effects of trauma. Resources are like assets—the more you have, the better off you are. Helping clients to identify the resources they already possess and develop the ones they lack is necessary to safe trauma therapy. Functional resources such as adequate locks, physical resources such as strength or coordination, psychological resources such as a sense of humor and defense mechanisms, interpersonal resources such as friendships, family, and pets, and spiritual resources including belief systems and communing with nature will all help in mediating trauma.

5. *Regard defenses as resources. Never "get rid of" coping strategies/defenses; instead, create more choices.*

Defense mechanisms are strategies for dealing with adversity. They are like old, dependable friends, helping us to deal with stress and getting us through hard times. The problem with them is that they tend to be one-sided, allowing only one choice for action. However, getting rid of a client's defenses doesn't solve problems and can actually increase them. Eliminating defenses robs clients of old friends and can leave them without coping strategies. A better alternative is to create additional, more adaptive defenses—new friends—so there are more choices of response. For example, instead of stopping a tendency to withdraw, pay attention to when it might be the best strategy, and simultaneously build skills for engaging with others. That way the client can decide for himself when it is best to be in the company of others and when it is better to be alone.

6. *View the trauma system as a "pressure cooker." Always work to reduce— never to increase—the pressure.*

Provocation is never a useful therapeutic strategy for those with PTSD. These individuals are already at the edge of how much they can handle. To further provoke a PTSD client's fragile system through confrontation or provocative interventions can further damage her; the possibility for retraumatization when using such interventions is great. It is much better to reduce pressure while increasing resources. That will enhance the possibility of opening up a fragile system without explosion (or decompensation).

7. *Adapt the therapy to the client, rather than expecting the client to adapt to the therapy. This requires that the therapist be familiar with several theory and treatment models.*

The trauma therapist who only has one therapy method to offer his clients puts them in jeopardy—no matter how great the model is. Many methods use techniques that are unappealing to some clients; others require ways of thinking that may be foreign. With only one kind of therapy on hand, the clients who, for whatever reason, do not fit with that method are at risk of additional harm through feelings of helplessness and failure.

8. *Have a broad knowledge of theory—both psychology and physiology of trauma and PTSD. This reduces errors and allows the therapist to create techniques tailored to a particular client's needs.*

Being versed in only one school of theory is like only being able to bake a cake from one kind of cake mix. A more tasty alternative is to keep a wide range of recipes and ingredients on hand. This makes it possible to create and choose the combination that is most appropriate at a particular time.

Knowledge is power. While no therapist can help all clients, the therapist who is familiar with a variety of theories has many clinical possibilities open to her. She then has the potential to create interventions uniquely suited to an individual client for a particular circumstance.

9. *Regard the client with his/her individual differences, and do not judge for noncompliance or for the failure of an intervention. Never expect one intervention to have the same result with two clients.*

When a medication fails to cure a patient it must be assumed that the correct one has not yet been found. The same applies to interventions or methods that fail to work with clients. The therapist must continue to look for or create an intervention or method that might succeed. It is important to avoid blaming the client by habitually thinking in terms of "resistance" or "secondary gain." Those terms imply that the client is impeding the success of the therapy—consciously or unconsciously—and that if he cooperated all would go well.

No two people are alike. A single method can work for many individuals, but it is demeaning to clients to assume that that will always be the case.

10. *The therapist must be prepared at times—or even for a whole course of therapy—to put aside any and all techniques and just talk with the client.*

It is great to have a broad collection of tools to work with in helping clients. However, there are occasions when the best thing we can offer clients is ourselves. I look back with embarrassment on situations in my early professional years when a client came to therapy with a pressing upset. Sometimes I was so quick to be clever with my tools that I would completely miss what was needed, often something as simple as listening. We do our clients a great injustice if we can only relate to them through our methods. For all clients sometimes and some clients all the time, the best therapy is just simple, unadulterated, human contact.

CHOOSING EFFECTIVE METHODS FOR CLIENTS

Outcome studies are valuable in that they offer basic guidelines, but they are limited to only a few of the available methods and can be misleading if taken at face value or viewed singly. An overview of research studies for trauma therapies reveals conflicting results, as many of the studies showing efficacy are disputed by subsequent studies and vice versa.

A recent article by Westen and Morrison (2001) casts light on both the advantages and limitations of outcome studies. They raise many important issues that need to be addressed if we are to better scientific research. One of their major points is particularly relevant to the topic of this book: the importance of distinguishing between *unsupported* treatment models and *untested* ones. The former have been shown to be deficient in some way; the latter have yet to be evaluated. That a method has not been proven in no way implies that it is flawed or unusable.

In the trauma field we have very few methods that have been studied and judged to be effective. We have many more methods that are still untested. That does not mean that we cannot use them, only that we need to apply them (as well as those that have been evaluated, for that matter) with caution, evaluating them as we go.

So how is one to choose an effective treatment for a particular client in the face of confusing outcome evidence for some methods and a lack of statistical evidence for others? The most obvious answer to that question involves common sense: *Ask your client*.

Rather than depending on outcome studies, help your clients to figure out for themselves what works best for *them*. Teach self-awareness, body awareness, and emotional awareness. Help your clients to ask questions such as: "When we are working in this way do I feel more calm? Do I feel more present? Is my life working better? Am I more resilient?" If the answer to those questions is primarily "yes," the direction you are going and the methods you are using are working well. However, if your clients are answering "yes" to: "Am I feeling more unstable, more decompensated, more spacy, less productive, or having more difficulty concentrating?" you need to try a different tack. In this way you both can evaluate *together* what works best.

Basically, the more models and approaches you have integrated in your practice, the more you can offer your clients. Begin by experimenting with one that seems promising for and/or appeals to your client, and then evaluate it. If it works well, continue with it; if it doesn't, try another. I often describe two or three methods to my clients and let them decide which seems best to try first. Make sure not to offer too many alternatives at once, as that can be overwhelming.

Another advantage of including clients in the decision-making process is that it gives them a greater sense of control over the therapy.

Remember, control is *always* compromised in trauma—trauma does not happen when one is in control—so the more you can give your trauma client a greater degree of control, the better.

CHOOSING A THERAPIST VS. CHOOSING A THERAPY

Every psychotherapist understands the importance of the therapeutic relationship. One of the risks of the current trend of competition among schools of trauma therapy is that the therapeutic relationship can suffer. With the emphasis on method, the relationship takes a back seat. This may work for some Type I and Type IIA clients. Yet for Type IIB clients—those for whom the therapeutic relationship is most important—the result can be devastating.

The importance of the contact between therapist and client is also ignored by the trend in managed care to limit the number of allowed psychotherapy sessions to sometimes as few as two. This is unfortunate, as it is the client who loses. In order to delve into difficult issues, expose vulnerable emotions, and tell secrets, a level of trust must be built. Moreover, when sessions are limited, the emphasis may be on resolving a traumatic situation or memory that a client is ill-equipped to address. Again, it is Type IIB clients who are most negatively affected by the limitations imposed by some managed care companies.

CHAPTER THREE

Overview of Theory and Treatment Models Applied in this Book

"There are many ways and means of practicing psychotherapy. All that lead to recovery are good."
—SIGMUND FREUD (1953)

This chapter contains a brief overview of the methods and theories applied in this book. Some of them are rooted in general psychotherapy and some are specific to work with trauma. I have chosen them because they are the methods with which I am most familiar. However, just about any theoretical model and method of psychotherapy or body psychotherapy can be adapted for work with trauma when it is combined with adequate amounts of common sense and a basic theory of trauma's effect on the body and mind.

SOMATIC TRAUMA THERAPY

Somatic trauma therapy is what I call the work I do, teach, and write about. I never set out to create a new model. My primary concern has always been to make trauma therapy safer. Somatic trauma therapy is an integration of the theories and models I have learned, peppered with occasional bits of original thinking and a liberal amount of common sense. Every therapy in this book is consistent with somatic trauma therapy, as are the exercises and cases in *The Body Remembers*. The basis for somatic trauma therapy is my concept of "putting on the brakes"—before and during work with traumatic memories.

BODY PSYCHOTHERAPY

There are many types of body psychotherapy, just as there are many types of psychotherapy. To identify oneself as a body psychotherapist, one must in some way consider the body as part of the psychotherapy process. Most body psychotherapists believe that integration of mind, body, and emotions is the major goal of therapy. However, how this goal is approached can vary widely. There are those who sometimes touch, hold, or otherwise physically comfort a client, and those whose major goal is emotional release. For a long time there has been a growing trend in the field of body psychotherapy to pay greater attention to the intricate function of the body, including the nervous system, muscular anatomy, visceral systems, etc., and the synergy between these systems and the mind.

Examples of body psychotherapies in this casebook are: somatic trauma therapy, Levine's SIBAM model, and the bodynamic running technique. Sometimes eye movement desensitization and reprocessing (EMDR) is also placed in this category because of the use of eye movements and the inclusion of body awareness in its protocol, but as of this writing, the EMDR Institute has no relationship to any body psychotherapy organizations.

PSYCHODYNAMIC PSYCHOTHERAPY

Psychodynamic psychotherapy is based on the idea that behavior is influenced by unconscious motives and feeling states. Gaining insight into this unconscious material is essential to change. It is the principle underlying psychoanalysis and many current psychotherapies, including many body psychotherapies. The major technique employed in psychodynamic psychotherapy is verbalization of the thoughts, feelings, and memories the client has—putting them on the table, so to speak—so that they can be looked at. Catharsis is believed to help this process by relieving the pressure of emotion and clearing the mind for more rational thought. The importance of transference and countertransference is also emphasized in psychodynamic psychotherapy.

In the field of trauma therapy we have many old and new therapeutic tools at our disposal; for some clients, the basics of psychodynamic psychotherapy are just right.

TRANSACTIONAL ANALYSIS (TA)

TA was developed in the 1950s by the psychiatrist Eric Berne (1961). As its name implies, it involves the analysis of interpersonal and intrapersonal communication. Adherents of Berne's TA coined the now-common terms *inner child* and *adult egostate*. The theory and concepts of TA were influential in the development of ego state therapy (Watkins, 1993), which is currently used in conjunction with hypnosis for the treatment of dissociative disorders (Phillips & Frederick, 1995). The emphasis in TA is on the interaction (transactions) among the *parent*, *adult*, and *child egostates*, whether between people or intrapsychically.

Particularly helpful in trauma therapy is the TA concept of *redecision* (Goulding & Goulding, 1979), where the client identifies decisions made during stressful times or traumatic events. Once decisions are uncovered, they can be looked at and "redecided" when appropriate.

The goal in using TA in trauma therapy is to develop a better inner relationship and dialogue, which furthers healthy adaptation and growth.

GESTALT THERAPY

Gestalt therapy was founded in the 1940s by the psychoanalyst Fredrik S. Perls. It was revolutionary at the time as it focused on the here and now, rather than seeking historical roots to personal problems (Perls, 1942). Practitioners of Gestalt therapy are interested in monitoring changes in all aspects of awareness, including body awareness, though Gestalt is not considered a body psychotherapy.

The most widely known aspect of gestalt therapy is the "empty chair" technique, popularized in films of Perls's work at Esalen Institute in the 1960s. Contemporary use of this technique is common among psychotherapists of many disciplines, as it is useful for making internal conflicts and dialogues concrete.

In trauma therapy, the gestalt therapy empty chair technique can be useful for projecting inner conflicts outward where they can be heard, viewed, assessed, and, hopefully, changed. It is a useful adjunct to transactional analysis in aiding the dialogue between egostates.

COGNITIVE BEHAVIORAL THERAPY (CBT)

CBT is a composite of several methods, all based on the principle that how we think influences how we feel and behave. The major goal of CBT is to change how the client thinks about his problem, whatever that may be: trauma, phobia, conflict at work, etc. Then, it is believed, changes in emotion and behavior will result.

Principles from CBT lie at the heart of most currently available trauma therapies. Actually, much counseling and psychotherapy has roots in one or more aspects of CBT, including cognitive therapy, assertiveness training, and relaxation training (Foa, Keane, & Friedman, 2000). Systematic desensitization, probably the best-known treatment for anxiety and phobias and the basis of CBT's method of exposure therapy, was originally developed by the father of behavior therapy, Joseph Wolpe (1958). Any method of trauma therapy that uses imaginal exposure (remembering all or part of a trauma as if it is occurring now) as part of the protocol—as most do—has been influenced by CBT.

A central but often bypassed contribution of CBT to trauma therapy is its emphasis on rational thinking. As the ability to reason and think clearly is often a casualty of trauma—both in its immediacy and in its aftermath—the cognitive therapy principles of CBT become integral to trauma therapy. They are most useful for mediating the influence of the client's belief system, self-concept, and thoughts on behavior in the aftermath of trauma. The somatic trauma therapy concept of *dual awareness* is inspired by CBT, as is EMDR's *cognitive interweave*.

CBT also alerts us to the importance of uncovering any decisions made during a traumatic event about self, life, and the future. Many therapies adapt this CBT concept, including TA *redecision* and the *meaning* element of Levine's SIBAM model.

EYE MOVEMENT DESENSITIZATION AND REPROCESSING (EMDR)

Developed during the 1990s by Francine Shapiro, EMDR is one of the newer models of short-term psychotherapy, and it has been particularly effective in championing an interest in short-term trauma therapy.

Originally developed for use with symptoms of PTSD, its repertoire has widened in the last few years to include working with other kinds of psychological problems. EMDR combines principles of CBT (exposure, desensitization, cognitive restructuring) and neuro-linguistic programming (NLP; reframing) with bilateral stimulation—that is, side-to-side eye movements. It is further enhanced by concepts from other psychotherapies.

EMDR is founded on the belief that the eye movements (or other kinds of bilateral stimulation such as tapping alternate knees, hearing alternating sounds in opposite ears, etc.) hasten integration of traumatic memories and " . . . facilitate a rebalancing or stimulation of the information-processing system" (Shapiro, 1995, p. 321).

Simply put, the EMDR protocol consists of a tightly structured procedure for processing a trauma. Shapiro prefers "to target the most upsetting incidents first" (1995, p. 75), suggesting that getting the worst over with reduces the anxiety of what could come later. Here, Shapiro and I disagree, as I believe many clients are not prepared to face the worst without preamble or practice. Often a safer strategy is to begin work with lesser incidents, the resolution of which can imbue experiences of success, a garnering of resources, and the boosting of courage to tackle the worst.

The EMDR protocol is used to identify the disturbing elements tied to a trauma: visual or other sensory image, the negative self-belief, and associated emotions and body sensations. I have found the emphasis on gathering the central elements of a traumatic experience, especially identifying the negative self-belief, to be particularly helpful to my clients—at least as integral, if not more so, than the bilateral stimulation.

LEVINE'S SIBAM MODEL

Levine's SIBAM model is not actually a therapy method itself but rather a theoretical construct that helps us to understand the phenomon of dissociation. However, it can easily be applied as a treatment tool in trauma therapy.

Basically, the acronym SIBAM stand for the aspects of any experience as identified by Levine: sensation (S), images (I), behaviors/movements (B), affects/emotions (A), and meanings/cognitive understanding (M). According to Levine's theory, those still troubled by traumatic incidents are likely to have one or more of these elements dissociated from their memories of those incidents—that is, disconnected from the other elements and from consciousness (Levine, 1992). The goal of any trauma therapy—whether with this method or any other—is to integrate all aspects of a traumatic experience, bring them into consciousness, and create a cohesive narrative.

The application of this model is fairly simple. Once the dissociated traumatic elements are identified, specific questions and directions can be employed to facilitate the association of those elements. This allows the traumatic memory to become a completed whole rather than a group of disjointed parts, making integration of the experience possible.

BODYNAMIC RUNNING TECHNIQUE

Designed as a physically active intervention (Jørgensen, 1992, 1993), the bodynamic running technique is equally—and in some cases more—effective when the client imagines running rather than making actual running movements. This variation makes the intervention accessible to a wider variety of clients, including those whose mental state, physical condition, or personal preference prohibit them from actually running. It also makes it more accessible to those therapists who might shy away from a physically active method.

The bodynamic running technique was developed as a way to awaken or reawaken the flight reflex and to create an internalized impression of being able to run to safety and security. It is particularly useful in resolving traumatic events where the client froze or where the flight reflex was not possible to engage. If employed physically, the mechanism of awakened flight is obvious, as the client makes actual running movements while lying prone (Rothschild, 1996/1997, 1997; Jørgensen, 1992). When the client sits still in a chair and imagines running, the effect on the flight reflex is not as clear. However, upon close observation, both therapist and client will notice small muscular contractions in the legs when the client imagines running. These contractions coincide with what Levine calls *intentional movements*—contractions that carry the same intention as actual movement (Levine, 1992). Research has shown that imaginal rehearsal can stimulate the same nerve pathways as actual movement (Gerardin et al., 2000; Jeannerod, 1995).

NEURO-LINGUISTIC PROGRAMMING (NLP)

Unlike most psychotherapies, NLP did not evolve through experimentation between therapist and client. It was born in the early 1970s from observation of the therapeutic process—a study of some of the most successful therapists of their day. The creators of NLP, Richard Bandler and John Grinder, set out to identify what these therapists were doing that made them successful in helping their clients. Bandler and Grinder wanted to identify, operationalize, and systematize the strategies, techniques, and interventions that worked. Operating from the premise that emotions were greatly influenced by sensory perception, they observed that perception could be altered either by changing the sensation and/or by changing the language used to interpret it. The most effective therapists were doing just that on an intuitive level. Bandler and Grinder (1975) then proceeded to map the process so anyone could follow and use it.

Applications of techniques from NLP are particularly useful in containing and healing PTSD. A major symptom category involves *intrusive images* (APA, 1994), which can be auditory or visual. These images appear unbidden, often set in motion by triggers from internal states or external cues. No matter how they begin, they are overwhelming and upsetting, often escalating to the extreme of flashbacks. A few simple techniques adapted from NLP can help clients to change intrusive images by actually changing the sensory input, giving them a tremendous sense of control over these intrusions.

ATTACHMENT THEORY

Attachment theory focuses on the psychological impact of interaction between people. It reminds us that a child's relationship with her primary caretaker (usually, but not always, the mother) is extremely important and has an enormous influence over later psychological functioning. Obviously, a healthy bond between child and caretaker is preferable to an unhealthy or absent bond.

In the last few years attachment theory has wended its way into just about every model of psychotherapy and trauma therapy, championed by the writing of Allan Schore (1994) and Daniel Siegel (1999), among others, on the neurobiology of attachment. At this juncture, attachment theory is both revolutionary and old hat. That is, this current wave of investigation, hypothesis, and writing is giving us a scientific, research-laden basis for ideas and phenomena that psychotherapists have always known through anecdotal evidence as well as intuitively.

Moreover, attachment theory is giving us neurobiological evidence that a healthy bond between therapist and client can substitute for a missing or dysfunctional bond in childhood. It reinforces the importance of the therapeutic relationship as a place where there is a chance to supplement what may have been missed, damaged, or incomplete in the early years. What that means for psychotherapy is that science is blessing what we have always known, that the therapeutic relationship can be a place of healing even without modern techniques.

Applying attachment theory in trauma therapy becomes particularly important with Type IIB clients, many of whom had dysfunctional, abusive, and/or neglectful caretakers. In such cases, developing a healthy attachment between therapist and client is a necessary prerequisite to addressing traumatic memories, especially early trauma.

PSYCHOPHARMACOLOGY AS AN ADJUNCT
TO TRAUMA THERAPY

Psychopharmacology is the psychiatric specialty that deals with evaluating the chemical bases of psychological disturbance. The primary role of the psychopharmacologist is to assess a patient's need for medication, prescribe the appropriate psychotropic drugs, and monitor the effectiveness of drug therapy. While I do not consider medication to be a cure for PTSD and other trauma-related conditions, I do believe that creative assessment and accurate prescribing can be extremely beneficial for some of those suffering from debilitating symptoms. A credible psychopharmacologist will work in cooperation and conjunction with the trauma therapist, helping to optimize the client's functioning so that psychotherapy can have a greater chance of success. Nonpsychiatrist readers are urged to foster colleageal working relationships with one or more trusted psychiatrists. Developing such a relationship before a crisis occurs is always easier than developing one in the midst of pressing need.

As knowledge in this field is evolving and changing almost daily, the gospel of medication for psychological conditions changes often. Readers are advised to keep abreast of progress and changes in the wisdom *du jour* through professional journals and the current edition of the *Physicians' Desk Reference* (PDR).

Part Two

INTEGRATED TRAUMA THERAPY:
MANY MODELS FOR MANY NEEDS

CHAPTER FOUR

Putting on the Brakes

SOMATIC TRAUMA THERAPY

The major concern of somatic trauma therapy is to make every therapy experience as safe as possible for the client. *Putting on the brakes* is a slogan for this principle. During every session it is advisable to apply the brakes periodically, adjusting the level of arousal to keep it low enough to facilitate hippocampal function. Without attention to this, otherwise good therapeutic work may remain unintegrated. Putting on the brakes in the course of a trauma therapy session will be illustrated in several of the transcripts that follow.

In some cases, the client will enter the therapy room in an already-hyperaroused state, the accelerator pressed to the floor. When that happens, the therapist needs to help the client to put on the brakes immediately, before any other work is done. The following transcript illustrates one application of these principles.

Paula* was in her mid-thirties, married with three children under 10 years old. Her mother, who now lived in a different state, was very aggressive and highly critical. When Paula was a child, her mother had sometimes punished her harshly. Now no longer at risk of physical punishment, Paula lived in fear of her mother's judgment and verbal abuse.

Paula came into the room with an extremely high degree of hyperarousal. Her heart was racing and she was shaking. The first task, before we could do anything else, was to help her to put on the brakes. That meant reducing the hyperarousal so that she could feel safer and could think clearly.

The following dialogue took place in the first 10 minutes of a session that occurred early in her course of therapy. Paula entered with a bowed head, sat crouched in her chair, and shook.

THERAPIST: You're really shaking aren't you?

PAULA: Yes, I sometimes shake a lot.

THERAPIST: I can see that. What does it feel like to shake so much?

PAULA: I don't like it.

Paula was not able to answer a general body awareness question, so I became more specific.

THERAPIST: What does your body temperature feel like? Is it cold or hot?

PAULA: I feel like I am freezing.

*To protect privacy and confidentiality, all identifying client information has been altered throughout the book. For the same reason, many of the cases presented are actually composites of several cases. In each instance I have endeavored to maintain the basic principles and thrust of the therapy being presented. For those cases that are not composites, permission to include the material has been obtained from the client.

THERAPIST: What happens to your heartbeat when you're shaking like that?

PAULA: It feels like it is going to jump out of my chest.

THERAPIST: It beats very fast?

PAULA: Yes.

THERAPIST: And what happens when I ask you a question about temperature and heartrate? Does it change your shaking at all? Is it just the same?

PAULA: It's just the same.

Sometimes anxiety symptoms reduce when the client focuses on them. This did not happen, so I needed to try other interventions to help Paula calm down.

THERAPIST: Do you know what you are feeling emotionally?

PAULA: Very frightened.

THERAPIST: Right now?

PAULA: Yes.

THERAPIST: Of me?

PAULA: Well, no, not you. I'm just scared.

I didn't think it was of me, but it is always good to do a reality check. If she had said yes, I would have asked what it was that I was doing that scared her. Of course, it is possible that a client would say "no" when I actually was scaring her, either consciously or unconsciously. Either way, further intervention will probably reveal whether it is me or something/someone else.

THERAPIST: Can you see me?

PAULA: (*nods*)

THERAPIST: Clearly?

PAULA: Yes.

THERAPIST: Tell me what you see. Describe me: What color are my eyes? What color is my hair? Am I having a good hair day or a bad hair day?

PAULA: Your eyes and hair are brown. I think you are having a good hair day. (*We both laugh a little.*)

As long as she was not scared of me, I could use myself to help bring her into the here and now. And if I could get her to laugh a little, so much the better. If she actually was scared of me, focusing on me would have raised her anxiety. In that event, I would have had her stabilize by describing the room.

THERAPIST: What happens to your shaking when you look at and describe me?

PAULA: It's less.

THERAPIST: So you know it's me here?

If arousal had increased, I would wonder who she was imagining in my place.

PAULA: Yes.

THERAPIST: Am I doing anything right now that makes you feel scared?

PAULA: No, but I'm still scared.

T: I'd like to suggest that we experiment with the distance between us. It may or may not make a difference, but it could be interesting to try. Would that be okay?

Strangely enough, distance can make a huge difference in the client's comfort level. But you won't know it if you don't experiment. Sometimes a client wants the therapist closer, but it is often increased distance that enables more calm.

PAULA: I'll try.

THERAPIST: Okay. I'd like to first try increasing the distance between us. We can always come back to this if it feels best to you, but let's try something different first. Would you like to move, or prefer it be me?

Giving the client a little control.

PAULA: You.

THERAPIST: Okay. I'll move back a couple of feet and you pay attention to what happens in your body. (*I move back.*)

PAULA: (*exhales*)

THERAPIST: You exhaled, did you feel that?

PAULA: Yes.

THERAPIST: And something else changed. Do you know what?

I was not attempting to make a guessing game, but when possible, I want the client's awareness to precede my feedback.

PAULA: I stopped shaking.

THERAPIST: Yes, I can see that. How does that feel?

PAULA: Much better, but I'm tired.

THERAPIST: Would you like me to move back a little more? I can—it's okay—I can always come back.

PAULA: Okay, try it.

THERAPIST: One more foot?

PAULA: Try two.

THERAPIST: (*I move back.*) What happens?

PAULA: I can breathe easier.

THERAPIST: Does your heartbeat change? Is it still very fast?

PAULA: No.

THERAPIST: It's slower?

PAULA: Yes.

THERAPIST: How much?

PAULA: Much slower. It feels almost normal now.

With this information I began to suspect that in the future it would be a good idea to help her learn to pay attention to boundaries with others in her daily life. We knew her mother was intrusive, but we had not had a concrete example of the importance of physical distance until now.

THERAPIST: Your arms had been shaking a lot, what do they it feel like now?

PAULA: Very tired and heavy.

THERAPIST: Warm, cold?

PAULA: Warm.

THERAPIST: Evenly warm or . . .

PAULA: Evenly warm.

THERAPIST: Both arms are the same?

PAULA: Yes.

THERAPIST: How about your legs and feet?

PAULA: They are cold and my feet are sweating.

THERAPIST: Do they feel strong or weak? If I told you to get up and walk right now would you be able to do it?

PAULA: They feel sort of weak.

THERAPIST: Let's try something just to see if we can make them feel stronger: Put a little weight on your feet so you get a little bit of tension in your thighs. Do it as if you would tip your chair back, but don't do that. The point is to just get a little thigh tension. Can you feel that?

Increasing muscle tone will often increase calm and containment. For some it also aids in "grounding"—the ability to be present in the here and now.

PAULA: Yes.

THERAPIST: What do your thighs feel like?

PAULA: They feel firmer.

THERAPIST: When your thighs start to get tired release the tension very, very slowly, and tell me how that feels.

PAULA: They feel stronger.

THERAPIST: And the rest of you?

PAULA: Even more calm.

THERAPIST: Now that your body and emotions are more calm, I'd like to know more about what you are thinking. What have you learned in the last few minutes that we have been working?

Now that she is calmer, it will be possible for her to think clearly. Asking what she has learned will help integrate the experience of the last moments. If she can conceptualize what has happened and why, she may be able to use that information with others in the future.

PAULA: I am calmer when you are farther away.

THERAPIST: Do you know why you shook less when you were describing me?

PAULA: I was concentrating on you and not thinking about my mother.

THERAPIST: Do you think when you came in that you were expecting me to act like your mother?

PAULA: I think I expect *everybody* to act like her. And we had just had a fight on the telephone before I came.

THERAPIST: That points the way for some work for us to do together, to help you to see that not everyone is like your mother, to be able to differentiate who you should be afraid of and who you can relax with.

PAULA: Yes, that's a great idea!

We proceeded to do that during the remainder of the session. With the brakes on, Paula's hyperarousal reduced, and she was able to think clearly. It then became possible to help her differentiate her mother's behavior from mine and that of others in her life. We went on to focus on Paula's ability for dual awareness to help her recognize she was now an adult who could set limits with her mother. Paula didn't feel ready to verbalize limits yet, but she liked the idea of working toward that goal.

CHAPTER FIVE

Out of Flashback, Into the Here and Now

SOMATIC TRAUMA THERAPY, COGNITIVE BEHAVIORAL THERAPY

To be able to put on the brakes, you must first get and maintain the client's attention in the here and now. Sometimes, however, that can be very difficult. Such was the case with 40-year-old Arthur. The strategies applied here to stop the flashbacks are mainly from somatic trauma therapy. I also applied CBT principles of cognitive therapy to help Arthur begin to think more clearly.

As a child, Arthur spent 2 years in a foster home where he was sometimes violently punished. For most of his adult life Arthur was able to put his traumatic experiences behind him; however after he was assaulted on the street 2 years ago he began showing severe signs of PTSD. A previous therapist assumed the assault upset him because of his history of abuse and worked to help him "relive" some of the early incidents. This led to uncontrolled flashbacks of his childhood punishment. Arthur switched to another, more conservative, therapist, who felt overwhelmed with the wealth of Arthur's emotion. The therapist sought ongoing supervision and asked that I see Arthur for one session on a consultation basis.

There were probably several factors that led to Arthur's current state of decompensation with flashbacks. "Reliving" a trauma in its entirety is not always helpful (Post et al., 1998), especially not for someone with as complex a background as Arthur's. Moreover, it is all too common for some therapists to bypass a current trauma in favor of an early one. Doing that can create a kind of internal split that promotes instability. The client can become confused: "I came in for help with this, but my therapist is more interested in that."

My only goal for this session with Arthur was to help him to stay in the here and now. Many clients believe that they can best solve their traumas by living in flashbacks even though they are terrifying and result in further decompensation. Though sometimes clients are initially skeptical of my approach of pulling them out of a flashback, most report feeling as though I threw them a lifeline and then towed them to safety. Sometimes the hauling in is very hard work.

I was introduced to Arthur by his therapist in the waiting room of his office. I had been asked to see Arthur there, with the hope that he would feel a bit safer than he might have at my office. He was shy and slightly anxious, as one would expect when meeting a new therapist. But he was oriented in the here and now and greeted me normally. However, when he sat down in the therapy room chair, his eyes rolled up and he began writhing in the chair. It looked to me as though he was pulled into flashback as soon as he sat down.

THERAPIST: (*with a firm, but not angry, tone*) Arthur, can you see me now?

He flashed a look at me, then reverted back to his internal world. I remained calmly insistent.

THERAPIST: Arthur, what color are my eyes?

ARTHUR: I'm thinking of my foster father.

THERAPIST: No Arthur, tell me what color *my* eyes are. Tell me, I know you can see them.

I wanted to keep Arthur in the here and now. Identifying me and other things in the room should help with that.

ARTHUR: Brown.

THERAPIST: Yes, that's right, and what about my hair?

ARTHUR: (*hysterically*) Why are you asking me this? I'm thinking about my father!

THERAPIST: Arthur, I don't want you to think about your father, I want you to be in this room and I want you to look at me because I don't want you to be as scared as you are. If you come in this room and if you stay here, you'll be less scared. What color are my eyes?

ARTHUR: Why are you asking again?

I was encouraged that he continued to be able to hear me and respond.

THERAPIST: Because I want to know if you can still see them, can you see them?

ARTHUR: Yes, brown.

THERAPIST: Yes, and my hair?

ARTHUR: Brown.

THERAPIST: And my shirt?

ARTHUR: Black.

THERAPIST: Right. What about your shirt, what color is it?

ARTHUR: Blue.

THERAPIST: And your shoes?

ARTHUR: Blue.

THERAPIST: You're wearing a lot of blue today aren't you? You were very scared a minute ago. Are you any calmer now?

ARTHUR: But I don't want to be calm. I want to talk about my foster father so you can help me. (*Goes off again into flashback.*)

THERAPIST: (*in a slightly louder and firmer tone*) No, Arthur. Don't think of your father now. You get too scared when you think of him. It's more than you can handle right now. Stay here in this room with me. Keep your awareness in *this* room. I know you can do it because you just did it a minute ago. Look at the clock. What time is it?

ARTHUR: Twelve past twelve.

A good sign. He was listening and could respond.

THERAPIST: Good! And is that the same time that's on the watch on your arm?

ARTHUR: (*looks*) Yes.

THERAPIST: Good. What kind of seat am I sitting on? Can you tell? Is it a chair? Is it a stool?

ARTHUR: Why are you asking me these questions?

I didn't mind him challenging me, as it kept his awareness in the room, in the now.

THERAPIST: Because I want your attention in this room right now. I don't want you to be thinking of the things that are making you so scared.

ARTHUR: (*appearing less scared but more irritated*) But that's what I wanted to talk with you about!

THERAPIST: First I want you to know that you don't have to get so overwhelmed. Do you like feeling so scared?

ARTHUR: No.

THERAPIST: It looks like you have no control. Is that true?

ARTHUR: Yes.

THERAPIST: Would you like to have more control over it? So that you can decide when it is a good time to feel that fear and when it is not?

ARTHUR: Yes, but I don't think that is possible, it just overwhelms me.

THERAPIST: I believe it is possible. I've helped other people do just that. Actually, that's what I'm doing with my questions. Do you feel any less scared when you have to focus on my questions to answer them?

ARTHUR: Yes, a little.

THERAPIST: You can feel that?

ARTHUR: Yes.

THERAPIST: What's different in your body?

ARTHUR: I don't feel it anymore here (*points at face*), but I still feel it here (*points at chest*).

THERAPIST: Okay, so it's less on your face, but not on your chest. It looks to me like you can breathe a little bit easier, though, is that correct?

ARTHUR: (*nods*) But there are those things that I would like to talk about.

THERAPIST: I'd like to talk about those things with you. But I would like to do it in a way that will help you resolve those memories so eventually they won't scare you anymore. That means a little at a time instead of all at once. Does that make any sense to you?

ARTHUR: Maybe, but I have to talk about my foster father (*voice goes up and he becomes upset again*).

I expected this to keep happening from time to time as I demonstrated to Arthur the advantage of staying in the here and now and explaining my rationale to him. This time he stayed in contact with me longer before going back to his flashback. I tried to increase those periods and help him notice the emotional and physical changes that accompanied them.

THERAPIST: Arthur, you've gone off again into your *memories*. See if you can bring yourself back to see me here.

It was important to label what was going on as a "memory" because a flashback can seem like current-time reality.

ARTHUR: I can't.

THERAPIST: Okay, I'll help you. Can you see me?

ARTHUR: (*glances*) Yes.

THERAPIST: Name two things you see when you look at me.

ARTHUR: Why are you asking me these questions?

THERAPIST: Answer my question first and then I'll answer yours. What do you see when you look at me?

I was negotiating to get him to focus on the here and now.

ARTHUR: You have brown eyes and brown hair.

THERAPIST: Good. Now I'll answer your question. As I told you before, I'm asking you these questions to help you be here in this room with me, and not sucked into your memories. What happens to your body when you answer my questions. Can you feel it change?

ARTHUR: (*reluctantly*) Yes.

THERAPIST: How?

ARTHUR: I shake less.

Arthur is beginning to be aware that his body feels different when he is in flashback and when he is present in the here and now.

THERAPIST: Yes, you are shaking less. That's why I'm asking you these questions—to show you that you can have some control over the fear, the shaking, and the trouble breathing.

ARTHUR: I can't control it. I remember my foster father's hands . . .

I was obviously not getting through enough. I needed to change my tactic, but first I had to get Arthur's attention again, get him back to the here and now.

THERAPIST: Arthur! Stop seeing that *memory*. Focus on what is in this room. Name three things.

ARTHUR: (*with irritation*) The big clock on the wall, the brown rug, the bookshelf over there.

He still went off, but he came back more quickly. That and his irritation are both good signs.

THERAPIST: Good, very good. What color are your shoes today? Look down and tell me.

ARTHUR: Blue.

THERAPIST: Now think: How long ago was it that you were in the foster home? You're not going to *remember* it, you're only going to *figure out* how long ago it was.

I wanted him to think. Figuring numbers was good for that. I was beginning to apply ideas from cognitive therapy, to help him toward objective observation.

ARTHUR: I don't know.

THERAPIST: What year was it?

ARTHUR: When I was 10.

THERAPIST: What year is this?

ARTHUR: Two thousand.

THERAPIST: How many years *ago* were you 10?

I emphasized "ago" to emphasize the past. I continued to do that until he could grasp that he was remembering, that whatever it was that was scaring him was a memory, not happening right now. I was also consciously not *asking him about what* it *was. I didn't want him to talk about it. To ask for details would have taken him further into the flashback and I wanted him out of it.*

ARTHUR: Thirty.

THERAPIST: And when did you leave that home?

ARTHUR: When I was 12.

THERAPIST: And how long ago was that?

ARTHUR: Twenty-eight years.

THERAPIST: Okay, so that was a long time ago. You're *remembering* something that happened 28 to 30 years ago. I want to help you learn the difference between *remembering* and feeling something that is happening right now.

ARTHUR: I don't know if I can do that.

THERAPIST: Well, I can understand your skepticism. You haven't been able to do that recently. But you were able to do it before. Didn't you spend a lot of years not being scared by that memory?

It was important to remind him of a resource he'd lost hold of.

ARTHUR: Yeah . . . I forgot. It was like I'd forgotten it.

THERAPIST: I'd like to try something I think will help; it's an experiment. Let's stand up and go over there (*gesturing to the other side of the room*). I'd like to talk with you there.

I wanted Arthur to step outside of the flashback state. I wanted to engage his reason, his adult. I wanted him to look objectively at what was happening, and he was not going to be able to do that while sitting in the same chair. I suspected that the "therapy chair" had become conditioned to be a place where he went out of control emotionally. If I was right, we would have a totally different contact standing across the room and talking—more like we had in the waiting room. It can also help to get someone who is overwhelmed by emotion to stand up, get the support of his legs and feet under him, make his muscles tense up and work. Emotional containment seems to be easier in a tense state than in a relaxed one.

ARTHUR: Why do you want to do that?

THERAPIST: I'll tell you over here. Come on. (*I got up and moved to the other side of the room where there were no chairs; Arthur followed.*) I want to talk about what was happening over there (*pointing back to the chairs*). I wanted to get you to "step outside" of that situation so you might be able to look at it more objectively. Okay?

ARTHUR: Is this a trick?

THERAPIST: Well, yes, to be honest, it is sort of a trick. But if it works, then it's a really good trick. The point is I want you to have more control. It looks to me like when you sit in that chair over there, you feel completely helpless in controlling your emotions. Is that right?

With all clients, and especially with a client like this, with whom trust is at such a premium, it is imperative to be honest and not to manipulate. It is also important to "lay all the cards on the table." I wanted Arthur to know exactly what I was doing and why. This would not only help to engage his trust, but also his ability to think, something he had been missing up until that point, at least in much of this session.

ARTHUR: Well, yes.

THERAPIST: Are you interested in having more control?

ARTHUR: Will that help me? Don't I need to keep feeling those feelings to get over them?

THERAPIST: Actually, from what you and your current therapist tell me, and what I am seeing now, I don't think that way of working is helping you. It seems to me that you have been trying for a long time to fully feel those feelings, but that you are getting more and more upset, and more and more dysfunctional. What do you think about that?

ARTHUR: I hadn't thought about it. Maybe that's true. But I thought if I just kept at it, that I would get better.

He is thinking better on his feet. It is a common misconception that staying with emotions is always beneficial. When staying with an emotion leads to integration, better function, and relief, it is a good idea. But when staying with an emotion leads to dysfunction, decompensation, and increased distress, it is absolutely not *a good idea.*

THERAPIST: I can't give you a guarantee, I can only tell you my opinion from my experience. It doesn't look like it is helping you. Expressing emotions can help, yes, but not when you can't tell the difference between a long time ago when something happened and today when it is not happening—when the memory feels like it is happening right now. Emotional expression in trauma therapy helps the most when you know that what you are feeling has to do with something that happened in the *past*. Tell me, how do you feel right now, standing here talking with me?

ARTHUR: Oh. A little shaky.

THERAPIST: Can you be more specific? What's happened with the trembling and your trouble breathing?

ARTHUR: I'm breathing okay, but my legs feel a little weak.

THERAPIST: So, could you say you feel any better?

ARTHUR: Yes . . . (*a little surprised*).

THERAPIST: Look back at the chairs over there and remember how you were feeling over there—*don't feel it*, just remember it, like watching a movie.

Here Arthur got a chance for a really objective look.

ARTHUR: Okay. I was very terrified and overwhelmed. It makes me sad to look over there and remember how upset I was, how upset I am a lot.

Sadness is a healing emotion, it means that the sympathetic arousal is reducing and the parasympathetic increasing—a good sign.

THERAPIST: That's fine. I can understand you would be sad remembering that. Why do you think you got so upset over there?

I wanted Arthur to think and make sense of what had been happening.

ARTHUR: I couldn't stop feeling like it was happening now.

THERAPIST: Do you see any benefit in how you are feeling now in comparison?

ARTHUR: Well, at least right now I know it is not happening.

THERAPIST: Good! I'd like to suggest, if you are willing, that you spend a week in that awareness and see how it goes. If you find that you don't like it or don't find it to be beneficial, you can always go back to the other. What do you think?

Choice is important for a sense of control. I never imply a client must change. Instead I suggest experimentation with new awarenesses or behaviors followed by an honest evaluation of the pros and cons. Homework is a common feature of cognitive therapy and very appropriate here, for Arthur.

ARTHUR: I think it might be hard; it's easy to slip into. But I would like to try it.

THERAPIST: What could you do to get back to the here and now if you do slip?

It would aid his thinking to plan ahead what he could do if he loses his grip on reality.

ARTHUR: I guess I could name things in the room, like you were making me do.

So all of that persistence paid off. He remembered it and saw it as a possible resource.

THERAPIST: Good idea.

ARTHUR: Will I never get to work through those feelings? I don't want to have them haunting me the rest of my life.

THERAPIST: Probably you will, if you can learn to manage when you go into them. When you are able to maintain the awareness that you are *remembering* something in the past, I think you will be ready. But it will take some time and practice before you get to that place. The idea is for the amount of emotion to get *smaller*. What you've been doing up until now by "reliving the past" has actually increased your emotion, making it more and more overwhelming to deal with. When you get good at knowing those feelings have to do with something in the past, the amount of emotion will gradually get smaller and eventually dissipate. That is when you will really resolve it. It will take some preparation, but then I think you will be able to do it. Meanwhile, your daily functioning is likely to improve as a side benefit.

ARTHUR: Okay, I'll try it for a week.

THERAPIST: Good. Let's talk together with your therapist about it. But for now, don't sit in that chair.

This session moved Arthur toward stabilization, a prerequisite for working with traumatic memories. Arthur's tendency to become overwhelmed so easily suggested that he might be the type of client who does not benefit from work with trauma memory. However, that did not turn out to be the case. Over the following months Arthur became more skilled at keeping his awareness in the here and now and containing his emotions. I suggested that once Arthur was stabilized, he might be ready to work on trauma. I advised his therapist to work first on the street assault that originally brought Arthur to therapy. I believed that successful resolution of that recent trauma could provide a firmer base for working on his early traumas. This proved to be true. At last report, Arthur was making his way through his traumatic childhood slowly and without episodes of decompensation.

CHAPTER SIX

Applying Transactional Analysis
in Trauma Therapy

TRANSACTIONAL ANALYSIS,
GESTALT THERAPY,
PSYCHODYNAMIC PSYCHOTHERAPY

The ability to think clearly and rationally and the ability to self-nurture are skills that are either weak or absent in many of those with PTSD. During a traumatic event reason may evaporate as hyperarousal suppresses the function of the hippocampus, and feelings of self-loathing and self-betrayal emerge because the trauma was impossible to prevent. It is also possible for PTSD to take hold because the individual never learned how to reason under stress and/or how to forgive human error and weakness. Whether lost or never developed, these resources are important to acquire and/or enhance with many clients at some time during trauma therapy. For some clients, that will be the bulk of the therapy.

I find TA to be quite useful in developing these resources, as it helps to improve the dialogue between egostates. For that, gestalt therapy's "empty chair technique," by which an explicit dialogue between ego states can be developed, provides a good framework.

PARENT, ADULT, AND CHILD — A BRIEF OVERVIEW

It is worth reviewing the TA conception of personality. Basically, there are three main egostates: parent, adult, and child. Each has unique features, thoughts, sensations, and functions.

The Child Egostates

The child egostate has two aspects: natural and adapted. The natural child is undiluted emotion. The natural child cries when hurt, laughs when happy, screams when afraid, investigates when curious, seeks contact when lonely. It is not concerned with propriety; it just is. The adapted child, on the other hand, develops in response to the demands of the environment and the needs of survival. It *adapts*, as its name implies. The natural child may eat an appealing desert if it is hungry, but will not eat even its favorite if it is not hungry. The adapted child might eat a desert when it is not hungry in order to try to soothe a feeling of deprivation or find a substitute for love.

The Adult Egostate

The adult is not emotional. It is the keeper of facts and the voice of reason and logic. It is matter-of-fact. Common sense resides in the adult. It is the adult who knows rules and regulations and keeps behavior within the law. It doesn't threaten or criticize; it evaluates cause and effect. The adult might decline a fattening desert after evaluating the risks to health.

The Parent Egostates

The parent egostate also has two aspects: critical and nurturing. As each name implies, the critical parent judges and criticizes whereas the nurturing parent nurtures. The critical parent will criticize poor eating judgment: "That was stupid of you to eat that—don't you know what it will do to you?" The nurturing parent might say, "I'd rather you not eat that because I care about your health and I want you to live a long time." However, in cooperation with the nurturing parent and adult, the critical parent can learn to set balanced limits: "I won't allow you to eat this because it will hurt your health."

ANITA: WHO'S DRIVING?

Anita was referred to therapy following her second car accident. She had begun to have panic attacks while driving on the freeway. Because the first consideration of trauma therapy is safety—both in the therapy room and in the client's daily life (Herman, 1992)—part of Anita's therapy was to take a look at her driving habits. Anita reluctantly admitted that she liked to drive fast and to challenge the speed limit, often exceeding it. She was an aggressive driver, frequently becoming frustrated or even outright angry when those in front of her hampered her progress. She was prone to tailgating and weaving in and out of lanes in an effort to move as quickly as possible. Both accidents had been the result of her impatience. As a first step towards resolving the emotional trauma of her accidents, she needed to learn to drive safely.

Confronting her driving habits was not going to be easy. Underneath a rough bravado, she felt ashamed. Whether that shame had to do with her reckless behavior or with getting caught was not yet clear. But shame is difficult to deal with under any circumstances. I waited a few sessions to broach the topic of her driving habits until she had gained some trust in me, and then I proceeded carefully.

When the time came, I taught her the basics of TA theory—the concepts of parent, adult, and child. Once she grasped the ideas, I asked her in a matter-of-fact manner which egostate she thought was usually active while driving. Evidently the approach was adequately nonthreatening, as Anita was quick to admit it was her child who usually drove. I then asked how her adult would drive differently. This was also easy for her. The adult would drive within the speed limit, never tailgate, and not swear or gesture at other drivers. How, I asked, would she feel about driving that way? She responded that she would be bored—the child egostate would be bored and, perhaps, angry. I persisted: Could she see any rationale in letting her adult drive sometimes? (Actually, this was a slightly manipulative question, as it was aimed at engaging her adult to answer it). Reluctantly, she admitted she could. At the very least, she noted, it would eventually get her insurance rates down—a big motivation.

Then we looked at what was going on in her parent egostate. Her critical parent was saying, "Do what you want; I don't care what happens to you." This was an attitude Anita had felt from her mother, who, as a single parent, was often overwhelmed. She also recognized it in herself. She was often reckless, heedless of consequences. Her nurturing parent egostate felt helpless to control the wild child. We both knew that before Anita could really deal with the trauma of her accidents, her panic attacks, and the neglect of her childhood, she would need to develop a stronger, more caring, nurturing parent. That was going to take a bit of time. As Anita wanted some immediate relief, and I was concerned for her safety, we decided to first utilize and strengthen her adult egostate.

The next step was to help Anita design and agree to a contract for safe driving. Contracts are commonly used in TA to facilitate changes in behavior (Goulding & Goulding, 1979). Making and sticking to a viable contract requires agreement of all three egostates: parent, adult, and child. Anita proposed having her adult drive to work and letting her child drive the rest of the day. She figured that would be the most challenging; she was the most impatient when she was still a little sleepy and feared being late for work. She also had had her last accident in the morning. The plan had a minor snag, though. Her proposal would require leaving home 10 minutes earlier, meaning she also had to rise 10 minutes earlier each morning. But since she was limiting the contract to only a week, she thought it manageable. Her child egostate thought it would be boring, but was willing to cooperate for one week. Her nurturing parent egostate liked the idea and hoped she would extend the term. Some TA therapists might criticize this contract, as it did not completely cover all aspects of safe driving. However, for Anita it was a big step forward. I wanted to make sure that whatever change she decided on was really possible to accomplish with minimal effort. The aim was to get the experience of changing habits off to a good start. It was my hope that with a success under her belt, making and holding future contracts for increased safety would be easier.

At the next week's meeting, Anita was feeling pretty smug. She had managed the new schedule and actually found that the traffic at the slightly earlier time was much lighter, making the drive to work more relaxed. She therefore arrived at work in a better mood, which positively affected her relationships to coworkers. Although predictably bored driving at the slower speed, her child enjoyed the reduced pressure at work enough to be cooperative in continuing the new morning schedule and pace. As an aside, she also told me that she had not had any panic attacks on the freeway that week.

Of course, it is not always this easy to help a client to change dangerous behaviors. But if you can accomplish change, the result is often similar to Anita's experience. The child is frequently relieved that someone competent is finally in charge and caring for her safety.

I hoped that eventually Anita would want to extend the contract to cover all of her driving. However, that needed to be approached more slowly. If imposed too quickly or under duress, the progress could backfire. With the success of this first intervention under her belt, Anita was interested to see what else might be helpful. She could see the benefits of strengthening her adult, and now also wanted to look at increasing the strength and activity of her nurturing parent egostate.

Self-nurturing

As discussed above, TA theory includes a distinction of parent and child egostates. There are a wide variety of disturbances possible in interaction between the distinct branches of both the parent and the child. The major aim is to quiet the critical parent and contain the adapted child so that a reconciliation can occur between the nurturing parent and the natural child. There are many variations on this theme. A current, popular one comes from EMDR therapist April Steele (2001), who has adapted the idea of a positive inner dialogue between parent and child parts into a procedure she calls *imaginal nurturing*.

TA practitioners often make use of the *empty chair* technique from gestalt therapy. The idea is to assign chairs to two or more egostates in order to help the inner dialogue to come out in the open. The therapist then aids the client in externalizing the internal dialogue by directing the interaction. The client speaks from the egostate assigned to each chair, moving around as the conversation develops. When conflicts are revealed, the egostates can discuss or argue until a resolution is reached. It is usually necessary to assign a chair to the adult, which is often instrumental in mediating disagreements. Through these dialogues, it is often possible to identify where the various voices, both positive and negative, originated—as internalizations of caretakers, creations from inner conflicts, resolutions of traumatic stress, etc. Once the dialogue is out in the open, it becomes feasible to quiet or disengage from those voices or attitudes that are no longer useful and further internalize the ones that are. Additionally, more constructive voices can be developed or strengthened. An example of this might be the creation of a healthy critical parent voice that warns or sets reasonable limits rather than condemning behaviors.

Sometimes the tide can be turned when it is revealed that a critical parent egostate is actually an adapted child in disguise. I have seen this happen many times. In playing out the different roles and giving each its own voice, what looks like "mature criticism" can actually have evolved as an attempt by a youngster to control his behavior to avoid disapproval from parents, teachers, or other significant adults. It can also develop following physical or sexual abuse—an expression of the common defense mechanism *identification with the aggressor.*

This is what proved to be the case with Anita. Her internal critical parent, the one who said, "Do what you want, I don't care what happens to you," was clearly an introjection of her mother's voice. She had been so overwhelmed taking care of two children while holding down a full-time job that she became outright neglectful.

Now, at times, Anita felt as helpless as her mother. She had no idea how to express caring towards herself or how to set and maintain protective limits. Her child egostate seemed to like being able to do as she pleased. But upon closer examination, she was also very scared—increasingly so after each accident.

During the time that Anita was developing her nurturing parent, she and I had several conflicts. The more she could feel that I genuinely cared about her, the more rebellious she became with me. This was a difficult time, as my own countertransference sometimes intruded and I was not always as patient with her challenges as I might have been. However, though she tested me mightily, she never quite pushed completely past any of the limits I set. And, when I could remember (in my own adult and nurturing parent) how frightened she must be to feel cared about after years of neglect, I was better able to tolerate and contain her outbursts and acting out.

Over several months, Anita was able to develop and strengthen her nurturing parent as she internalized parts of mine. Once that process got under way, she was actually able to remember a few nurturing figures from her childhood—a teacher, a neighbor, several friends—that she now could use to further evolve her own nurturing parent.

Once her adult and nurturing parent were strengthened, we went on to work with the trauma of her accidents (and several childhood incidents) using other methods. TA was the basis for building a firmer foundation under her so that she could tolerate the potentially unsettling work of trauma therapy.

HARRY: EVALUATING REALITY

Many traumatized individuals develop a severe split between what van der Kolk (1994) calls the *experiencing self* and the *observing self*. The experiencing self is closely linked to the brain's implicit processing system, evaluating reality on the basis of what is felt, mainly emotion and body sensations. The observing self is linked to the brain's explicit processing system, judging reality on what is perceived through the external senses. Usually "reality" is judged through recognizing and reconciling these two selves. But those who are severely traumatized may rely too much on one or the other.

One of the ways to bring these two selves back into a healthy balance is by creating a *dual awareness*, bringing attention to the self that is being ignored while not negating the one that has been dominant. Often this can be done by asking a client to simply acknowledge both realities—for example, "I am feeling scared *and* as I observe my environment I can see that I am not in any danger." With Harry, however, this was not enough.

Harry was constantly scared and saw danger everywhere. He continually defined reality according to his experiencing self—his internal, primarily sensory, experience of anxiety. Because he felt the sensations of fear constantly, he concluded the world was a frightening and dangerous place.

Harry grew up as the only child of alcoholic parents. Though never physically abused himself, he witnessed a great deal of violence, as his father regularly hit and berated his mother when drunk. At 28, Harry was chronically anxious, and because of that he often felt stupid and ashamed. He was unable to enjoy his growing success in the world of advertising. Though he remembered his traumatic past, he was unable to connect those events to his current state of instability.

During our first session, I took a thorough history. I asked Harry what gave him the most difficulty in his life. Clearly, it was his anxiety. Every bit of the world scared him. Though he went to work daily, it was always an effort to leave home. He rode his city's subway system with trepidation. He constantly worried about what he ate, fearing allergic reactions and food poisoning. The potential for physical ailments concerned him, but at the same time, he feared going to the doctor.

What pushed him to psychotherapy was seeing a TV movie about the eccentric recluse William Randolph Hearst. Harry feared that if he didn't do something while he was still young, he could end up like Hearst.

While it seemed evident that there was a link between childhood trauma and Harry's current anxiety disorder, he was too fragile to begin with work on those memories. He needed more stability and at least a beginning feeling of safety in his daily life before we could look at his past. First it was essential that he be able to live in the present.

We tried elements of CBT and NLP without success. Although often helpful in developing dual awareness, they made no impact on Harry. When we tried TA he readily grasped the concepts. When I taught Harry the basics of the theory, he quickly determined that his child egostate was associated with his experiencing self, with his anxiety and fear, and the adult egostate was associated with the observing self. He agreed that his adult egostate was rather impotent in many areas, especially in finding safety. He was primarily identified with his child egostate, which was also integral to his success in the advertising world; it was the source of his creativity and wit. At first, Harry was a bit concerned that building a stronger adult egostate might decrease his contact with his child egostate and thereby compromise his career success. But I was fairly confident that wouldn't happen. I reassured him that the goal was to build a healthy balance in his internal communication, to increase his ability to evaluate his external environment and soothe his fears, and to support the child egostate, not silence it. As with any other method, I suggested we try it out for a short time and then he could evaluate whether he liked the results or not.

We began by placing chairs in the room to represent his child, adult, and parent egostates. Harry moved among the chairs as he externalized his internal dialogue, making it explicit with words. The first dialogue involved the child and adult discussing how he felt in the therapy room at the current moment. The parent egostate was called upon to support both, particularly the child. The actual dialogue was quite lengthy, but the essence of it was quite simple:

CHILD: I'm really scared here. I don't feel safe.

ADULT: There is no danger in this room. Babette is sitting calmly in her chair and not moving. Nothing else is happening here, right now.

PARENT: (*to the adult*) That's great that you can accurately see what is happening here now.

PARENT: (*to the child*) Even though there is no danger right now, it is okay for you to feel afraid.

CHILD: Does that make me crazy to feel afraid when there is no danger?

PARENT: No. It is okay to feel what you feel. Feelings don't always make sense.

As this work developed, Harry began to realize that his fear was valid, but that it did not always have to do with the context in which he was feeling it. This made it possible for Harry to begin to glimpse where his feelings and sensations of fear might actually spring from. Slowly it dawned on him that they had roots in his traumatic past. This realization, bolstered by stronger adult and nurturing parent egostates, set a safer foundation for proceeding with therapy aimed at specific traumatic incidents from his childhood.

CHAPTER SEVEN

Emphasizing Resources

SOMATIC TRAUMA THERAPY, COGNITIVE BEHAVIORAL THERAPY

Accessing and utilizing resources is an imperative adjunct to any trauma therapy. In some instances, this can be sufficient therapy in itself. In the case presented here, resources were accessed to improve coping. Esther, 35, was participating in a professional training in a city she had lived in a few years ago. During that time she had suffered several unresolved traumas. Being back in the city was a trigger for her and made being at the training difficult. We conducted a mini-session, not to cure the traumas but rather to help her better cope with being in that city.

The major strategies used were based in somatic trauma therapy. Body awareness and resources were used to put on the brakes. We also identified past and present resources from her life and superimposed them on her impressions of the traumas. This helped to stabilize Esther's state of mind. CBT was adapted for two purposes: first, to increase Esther's capacity to think, and second, to apply a very quick exposure to her past.

ESTHER: Being here (*meaning Cedar Creek*) upsets me very much.

THERAPIST: In what way?

ESTHER: I've been anxious since I got here. I feel like I can't breathe. It makes it difficult to focus on the course.

THERAPIST: You have a history here?

ESTHER: I lived here for four years. I left three years ago.

THERAPIST: So as we start to talk about it, what happens in your body?

Already I wanted to assess her reactions. Often just naming something upsetting will raise arousal. It made for a good opportunity to begin body awareness training and establish a gauge.

ESTHER: I notice my breathing is shallower as we talk. (*pause*) Did I mention my heartbeat?

THERAPIST: No.

ESTHER: It's beating a little quicker.

Her coloring was good. There is a slight rise in SNS arousal, but it was not significant. I felt safe to go on.

THERAPIST: Think briefly about what happened here. Just the titles, no details.

At this point I didn't really need to know about what happened, as the goal is containment, not resolution. Moreover, I didn't want her to go into any detail. Usually, the more detail, the greater the arousal. We would not be working directly with the traumas anyway, because she was a student in my training, not my client, and because our time was limited to a single session.

ESTHER: Okay.

THERAPIST: What happens in your body when you think about it?

ESTHER: I feel tearful and sort of hot.

Although upsetting, these are basically PNS signs, meaning we can safely go forward.

THERAPIST: Do you know why this is so hard for you?

ESTHER: Part of me doesn't want to touch it, it's too awful. I've been avoiding coming to Cedar Creek. But now I am confused. Since arriving a few days ago, I've been having positive experiences, and I am also beginning to remember positive things, too, from when I lived here. I'd totally forgotten positive things from here.

THERAPIST: So you've had some bad experiences here and some good experiences?

ESTHER: Yes, bad experiences were the first two years I lived here (*her hands move towards the right*). The good experiences came in the last few days, and memories of the last year I was living here (*hands move to the left*).

THERAPIST: As you say that, how do you feel?

I was also curious about whether she would mention her hand movements.

ESTHER: For some reason this side of my head (*points to the right side*) feels cooler. And I am getting anxious.

Her arousal was continuing to rise slowly, so I was beginning to think about putting on the brakes. Body awareness previously had been calming for her, so I tried that again.

THERAPIST: Just now you moved your hands to the right when you were talking about the bad things that happened and to your left

when you mentioned the good things. Do you remember doing
that?

ESTHER: (*laughing*) No, I wonder why I did that?

*I didn't know either, but I was glad to engage her curiosity—one of the greatest
resources of psychotherapy. A curious client is open to experimentation and
exploration.*

THERAPIST: Are you aware of any difference between the right side of
your body and the left, in addition to the coolness in your head?

ESTHER: There seems to be a shift in weight going to this side (*showing
her left side*), like sand tipping over, and . . . and this side (*right*) is
expanding (*she giggles*). It's like putting water into a sponge.

THERAPIST: How does that feel?

ESTHER: I am feeling much calmer.

The body awareness is working to decrease her arousal.

THERAPIST: How do you know that?

ESTHER: I can tell by my breathing and my heartrate. Both are much
slower.

*So we successfully put on the brakes by using body awareness. Esther has a
highly developed sense of her body, which makes this work easier. She was ready
to move forward a little.*

THERAPIST: If you think about being in Cedar Creek right now, what
happens in your body?

*I was not interested in her remembering anything detailed that happened here,
but I wanted to assess what happened when the general thought of the city was
triggered.*

ESTHER: A slight swirl in my head like a panic. I also got a sense of the firmness of my back, but it is difficult to breathe.

It sounded like a mixture of anxiety and containment. I was encouraged to hear she felt firm in her back.

THERAPIST: Name a couple of the good things that happened in Cedar Creek.

It was time for her to remember some resources.

ESTHER: I forgot (*laughing*) . . . new friendships . . . the botanical garden . . . the sense of relaxation in that beautiful place.

THERAPIST: What happens to your body as you name those things?

ESTHER: It gets warmer.

THERAPIST: A pleasant warmer or . . .

ESTHER: A pleasant warmer.

THERAPIST: So you were a bit cool before?

It is common to not be aware of a sensation until it changes. This sometimes also happens to me as an observer; I suddenly notice color when I hadn't been aware that the face was pale.

ESTHER: Yes, but around here, I was a bit hot (*points at arms*). I can also feel my legs now. They feel quite strong and sturdy.

She sounded pretty solid, so I thought we could try something a bit more risky.

THERAPIST: I'd like you to imagine taking a flashbulb picture, a really quick glimpse, of your negative association to Cedar Creek and seeing what happens in your body.

This is a form of highly measured exposure à la CBT. I only wanted her to get a tiny taste.

ESTHER: Do you want me to describe what I see?

THERAPIST: No, you can't do that fast enough. I want it to be a really quick flash. No more than a "click," like the opening and closing of a camera's aperature.

ESTHER: Okay, I did it. Whew, I get a shiver, really deep, a slight panic.

THERAPIST: Tell me a little bit about the botanical garden.

This quick switch called on a positive experience of the city, positive resources, which could be superimposed on the negative ones on both an emotional and somatic level.

ESTHER: There's a wonderful tree and its branches are so wide it has to have supports to lean on. There are fantastic trees there, I've never seen anything like it before.

THERAPIST: Are there any of those new friends you would like to go with to the botanical garden?

I brought in human resources.

ESTHER: Yes.

THERAPIST: What happens in your body?

ESTHER: Warmth, especially in this hand (*points to right hand*) and up until about here (*upper right arm*).

THERAPIST: What happens to that panic about your negative associations to Cedar Creek?

ESTHER: A very small echo.

THERAPIST: What percent of Cedar Creek has good associations?

This kind of subjective gauge can be quite useful, though I forgot to get a rating at the beginning. It would have been a good idea, but the gauge was still useful. Because she was having so much difficulty being in Cedar Creek, it was probably initially more than 50% bad.

ESTHER: Now? 70%.

THERAPIST: Is that an improvement?

ESTHER: Oh, yes!

THERAPIST: How does that feel?

ESTHER: I've got a feeling of satisfaction. The most tension was here (*behind the neck*), which has moved away. I feel like there's a space in the back of my neck, and a sense of reality, of being present.

THERAPIST: How do you know that? What else happens in your body?

ESTHER: Well, it is like I can just feel my body more, and see you more clearly.

THERAPIST: What memories do you have of Cedar Creek in *this* year?

ESTHER: Lots of positive things. And I can remember more positive things from then, too.

THERAPIST: So it wasn't all bad?

ESTHER: No, but the bad outweighed the good in my memory.

She was able to think much more clearly and reflect on the meaning of her reactions.

THERAPIST: What are some of the good memories?

ESTHER: My work, my colleagues, I really developed in my profession, a lot of support and encouragement.

THERAPIST: How do you feel about it as you remember?

ESTHER: (*rubbing her stomach*) A really big belly (*laughs deeply*), and a sense of warmth. I also feel unfinished.

THERAPIST: Well, you do have a shadow here. Our work now was to help you get connected to your resources, not to resolve the old issues. So those are still there to work on with your own therapist. What are you thinking about now?

ESTHER: Before, being in Cedar Creek was about being here for other people. I really wasn't with myself then. My experiences became better when I was more connected to myself.

As her thinking cleared with reduced hyperarousal, a valuable insight came through.

THERAPIST: Is your breathing better now? It looks like it.

ESTHER: Yes, I can breathe quite deeply. Thank you.

THERAPIST: You're welcome.

It is not always necessary to directly address traumatic memories in order to contain them. In this instance, Esther benefited from identifying her somatic reactions and accessing resources associated to her memories. She never even had to reveal any details of the traumas. The results of the session were better than either of us expected. Upon returning to Cedar Creek both 6 months and a year later, for the following two trainings, Esther reported absolutely no discomfort at being there.

CHAPTER EIGHT

No Techniques Required

FOLLOWING THE CLIENT

Sometimes the best therapeutic technique is no technique at all. As mentioned earlier, with nearly all clients some of the time, and a few clients all of the time, techniques and methods are best laid aside. In those instances, at best they will not be useful, at worst they could do real damage. There are times when the intervention of choice must be to just be with the client, human to human, making contact, but following behind, not leading or interpreting. With a bright and skeptical teenager, this can be especially important.

Contrary to common wisdom and my usual routine, with extremely frightened clients I postpone history-taking until they feel more comfortable. Sometimes this takes several sessions. Following is a transcript from an initial session I had with one such new client.

Patti's anxiety could be heard in her voice even on the phone. At 18, she had never been in therapy before and was terrified at the prospect. However, her life had gotten to the point where she felt she had no choice. Her family doctor had offered her medication, but that scared Patti even more, as she was afraid to feel the effect. On the phone she alluded to a history of traumatic events but did not specify what they were. Because she was so anxious, I didn't press for more information. She suffered from severe anxiety and often had panic attacks. A freshman in college, she was afraid she might have to drop out. I discussed the usual things, office location, fees, and so on; I told her that I usually get a history during the first session. She agreed to that framework and we set a time.

When I greeted Patti in my waiting room she was pale, shaky, and mostly looking down at her feet. She only glanced at me before following me into my therapy room.

Patti entered the room and stood looking at the floor. She didn't seem to know what to do. I told her where I usually sit and suggested that she could stand or sit wherever else she wanted (I have a fairly large office with several seating choices). After a minute or so, she chose one of the chairs farthest from mine. I sat and observed her. Mostly she looked away. I spoke to her slowly as I did not want to further frighten her, and waited as she took her time to answer so that she could set the tempo. The pace of the dialogue was relatively slow, with periods of silence between each line.

THERAPIST: You seem pretty nervous.

PATTI: (*looking at her feet*) I am.

THERAPIST: Do you know why?

PATTI: I'm always nervous.

THERAPIST: Right now, do you think you are more nervous than usual or less?

I was not going to ask her about her body sensations at this point in time. She had just walked in the door and was scared to death. I wanted to follow her as much as possible, including using her language. It was not time to introduce my "method." Already I was thinking that I would not be able to get a history from her today because she was just too frightened. My goal became seeing if there was any way to help her be more comfortable.

PATTI: Maybe more than usual.

THERAPIST: Is there anything particular about the idea of being here that makes you feel more nervous?

PATTI: I'm afraid to feel even worse.

THERAPIST: Do you think you would feel worse if you looked around?

PATTI: I don't know. I'm afraid to look up and see you looking at me. I can feel your eyes on me.

THERAPIST: It doesn't sound like it feels good when I look at you.

PATTI: No, it doesn't.

THERAPIST: I'm going to look away for a minute or so. Tell me if that makes any difference.

I looked at a poster on my wall. I could see out of the corner of my eye that Patti looked up at me. I waited a while.

THERAPIST: Is there any difference?

PATTI: Maybe a little. But don't you need to look at me?

THERAPIST: Actually, I don't. If you are more comfortable when I look away, that's fine with me. If I need to know something, I can always ask you. I'm happy for you to make the call.

I wanted Patti to feel that she could have some control in the situation. I still had no idea about her history, but I was beginning to suspect themes involving control and shame. When a client has such severe difficulty being looked at, shame is often an issue.

PATTI: I'm afraid that if you say you will do that, that you might suddenly look at me when I'm looking at you.

THERAPIST: Well, what can I tell you about that? I have done this with other clients. It's one of the reasons I have posters I like, so I have other things to look at when the need arises.

PATTI: (*She looks at the posters on the wall, but she doesn't say anything.*)

THERAPIST: So, I am fairly good at keeping my eyes averted when asked, though not perfect at it. It would be my intention to keep my eyes off of you if you wanted that, but it could happen that a noise or sudden movement would cause a reflex glance. It wouldn't be on purpose to trick you, but it could happen.

With such a scared and skeptical client it is not a good idea to promise that I can do anything 100%. I want to leave latitude in case I make a mistake, to reduce the chance of her feeling intentionally tricked.

PATTI: (*keeps looking around*)

THERAPIST: Do you have any comment on what I've said?

PATTI: I don't know if I can trust you.

THERAPIST: Of course you don't, you just met me. I hope you won't expect that of yourself.

PATTI: I thought I had to trust you if you are going to help me.

THERAPIST: Trust is something that develops over time. You can't require or legislate it. The most you could expect is to see if I seem the kind of person you might be able to grow to trust eventually.

PATTI: Okay.

THERAPIST: I want to ask you a question. But I want to preface it by telling you that you don't have to answer my questions.

I wanted to point out that she had some control.

PATTI: But if I don't answer your questions, how can you help me?

THERAPIST: Well, you will probably find that some of my questions feel okay to answer and some don't.

PATTI: Don't you want to hear about my history, like you said on the phone?

THERAPIST: I'd rather you feel a bit more comfortable with me and being here first. Would that be okay with you?

PATTI: Um . . . I guess. . . . But then what?

THERAPIST: As I said, I'd like to help you be less uncomfortable here.

PATTI: How?

THERAPIST: To start, we could talk about how to reduce your anxiety in this room. Do you have any ideas?

Actually, I believed she was a bit calmer, as there was less time lag between my questions and her answers, and I could hear her breathing a bit more deeply. She was also looking around more.

PATTI: I don't know.

THERAPIST: Okay. What do you usually do when you come to a new place, to get familiar with it?

PATTI: Sometimes I look around.

THERAPIST: Do you do that sitting or standing or walking?

I wondered if it would help her to move around.

PATTI: I might get up and look around, at things on the wall and stuff.

THERAPIST: I don't know if you want to now, but that would be absolutely fine to do here.

PATTI: You wouldn't mind?

THERAPIST: No, not at all.

PATTI: Will you watch me?

T: Not if you don't want me to. But I suppose you know I can see you a little out of the corner of my eye.

Before I gave her carte blanche, I made a quick scan of the room and my desk to make sure there were no confidential papers or files lying around. I'm usually pretty conscientious about that, but I wanted to make sure.

PATTI: (*Gets up and begins to move around.*)

She was very tentative and stiff. Her posture was also slightly stooped. She moved slowly toward a poster on my wall.

PATTI: What's this? What's it say?

She was looking at a poster I had from Denmark. There was a black cat lapping milk from a bowl as it eyed a yellow canary sitting on the bowl's opposite edge.

THERAPIST: It's an advertisement for a Danish insurance company. There's a play on words. The name of the company is "TRYG" which means "SAFE." The caption says, "It's about feeling SAFE."

PATTI: Yeah. Brave bird.

THERAPIST: Do you think it's feeling safe?

PATTI: Looks like it. It isn't about to fly away.

THERAPIST: Why do you think it dares to stay there?

PATTI: (*She looks at it for a while.*) I think it knows the cat likes milk better, so it's safe as long as there is milk in the bowl.

THERAPIST: You know, I think you are right.

PATTI: (*She smiles a little and then starts to move around a bit more. She seems slightly more agile.*)

THERAPIST: How is it to look around?

PATTI: It's okay.

THERAPIST: How is your discomfort right now, any change from before you got up?

PATTI: Maybe slightly better.

THERAPIST: What does that tell you?

PATTI: I don't know what you mean.

THERAPIST: Well, if you are feeling slightly better now than when you were sitting, what might account for that? If you can figure it out, you might be able to either increase whatever it is, or do it again another time.

PATTI: I guess it helps to walk and to look around . . . (*pauses pensively*)

THERAPIST: Anything else?

PATTI: Maybe. The poster with the bird.

THERAPIST: Does that mean something to you?

PATTI: I don't know.

Or maybe she did, but she was not ready to tell me.

THERAPIST: Maybe you can think about that. But we have to stop soon, we only have a few more minutes. Let's talk about what we do next. Do you know if you would like to come back?

PATTI: Yes, I think so.

THERAPIST: Okay. Then let's make an appointment.

Which we did. She wrote out and handed me a check, thanked me, and walked out the door before I could rise to see her out.

We had a long way to go, but I was satisfied with this first session. Truth be told, at the outset Patti was so scared I did not know if she would be able to last the whole hour, and I was unsure about how to make contact with her. She surprised me, though. Many clients had asked about the poster, but none had made such a connection with it. For a first session with someone so scared, I believed it went well. But I correctly predicted this would be an arduous therapy.

CHAPTER NINE

Victimizing the Self

TRANSACTIONAL ANALYSIS, GESTALT THERAPY, PSYCHOPHARMACOLOGY

Among other things, encountering traumatic incidents can greatly influence one's self-concept. Particularly when trauma is at the hands of other people, being a victim can become part of the self-perception. Repeated episodes of mistreatment can also increase vulnerability to further victimization. It is not because the individual wants to be victimized or goes looking for it. Rather, she is missing or has lost the tools (reactions and resources) she needs to prevent it. The resulting victimization can be so pervasive that the individual ends up feeling internally victimized by herself.

TA's conception of internal dialogue among egostates and gestalt therapy's empty chair technique can help to (re)establish a beneficial (peaceful, friendly) relationship with the self. In addition, TA redecision theory (Goulding & Goulding, 1979) will be shown to be helpful in identifying and changing decisions and resolutions made under circumstances of extreme stress.

Roberta, an electrical engineer, came for therapy because of a depression brought on by a failed attempt at promotion. She further suffered from anxiety and low self-esteem, complaining of being unable to be assertive either at work or at home.

The early years of Roberta's life sounded fairly good—comfortable and stable. Her father worked in sales, and her mother stayed at home to care for the house and children. Mostly, the family got along well; there seemed to be plenty of love and attention to go around. Mother and father were a consistent parenting team. The usual assortment of childhood trials and tribulations were unworthy of note. Roberta had plenty of friends, was a good student, and liked school.

At age 9 Roberta was diagnosed with leukemia. From what she describes, the disease was much harder on her parents than on her. Typical of the chronically ill child, she became the emotional caretaker, attempting to spare her parents additional suffering, worry, and concern for her. Though often scared and in pain, Roberta went to great effort to minimize outward signs of distress. She taught herself to force a smile and to ignore her feelings. Often people dissociate when experiencing repeated trauma. Roberta didn't dissociate; instead she learned to endure. Eventually she made a complete recovery—physically, that is, but not emotionally.

Though Roberta admitted that the repeated hospital stays and chemotherapy were bad, the most damaging part of her experience with leukemia was having to confront her peers in a weakened and hairless condition once she was deemed well enough to return to school. Fourth grade is not a good time to be different or look different. She went from being a well-integrated member of her peer group to being an outcast, the brunt of intense teasing. As she progressed in school, difficulty with peers continued, and she was often victimized by scapegoating and bullying.

For obvious reasons, Roberta felt that her life totally changed when she became ill. She found her escape in mathematics. She excelled in her studies, finally settling on a career in engineering. However, the pattern of being scapegoated continued into adulthood. She was victimized at work and harassed in her marriage. Both her boss and husband were in the habit of verbally abusing her, and she felt helpless to do anything besides take it.

Roberta also came to feel victimized internally. She was terribly self-critical, prone to thinking of herself as dumb and stupid. She ridiculed herself for any size or kind of misstep.

Prior to her last failed attempt at promotion, the inner battering had been tolerable. But it had since mushroomed out of control and resulted in a severe depression. She still went to work daily, but did little else. She was loosing weight and having difficulty sleeping. On the job, her energy level was so low she was not able to keep up with her assignments and was falling behind.

FIRST STEPS

After taking a thorough history, the first order of business was referring Roberta to a competent psychopharmacologist. I believed that psychiatric confirmation of trauma-related major depression was in order. If I was correct, medication might be a good idea. There are situations where the right psychotropic drugs can be a terrific adjunct to psychotherapy and trauma therapy, and Roberta's was one of those. She needed to get some relief from the depth of her depression before she would be able to make use of what I could offer.

The psychopharmacologist concurred with my assessment. He prescribed an antidepressant and met with Roberta regularly to follow her progress and adjust dosage. While she was adjusting to her medication, our weekly sessions focused on daily stabilization. We knew when the dosage was well regulated, as her inner critical voices were quieted (but not silenced) and her energy level increased. This made it possible for us to proceed. We both realized, and discussed from the outset, that this would probably not be a short-term therapy.

SETTING THE STAGE

Roberta saw two related difficulties. She was extremely vulnerable to criticism from others, and she was equally vulnerable to criticism from herself. Intellectually she knew that she had a lot to offer. In therapy she could openly question why her husband stayed with her and her boss did not fire her if they thought she was such an "imbecile." But there was no way she could even consider asking them. She could, however, ask herself, and we decided to help her do just that.

Because Roberta wanted to consider how she talked to herself, I suggested that TA might be an excellent vehicle. It seemed obvious that she had a severely critical parent egostate and a very sad and depressed child egostate. Moreover, at least in the business world, she had a well-functioning adult, and in getting to know her, I found her to have a large supply of common sense. We also had the benefit of the security of her early childhood to tap into—a happy child egostate lurking in the background somewhere. And there was certainly a nurturing parent internalized from her years of good parenting. Those egostates might be lying dormant, but I was sure they were not dead—they were resources waiting to be awakened and utilized.

Because of her history of external and internal criticism, I suggested that somewhere along the line she might feel criticized and/or abused by me. With her background, the likelihood of that happening was high. I further suggested that having such a conflict between us might even be desirable, as it could provide fertile ground to learn to handle those issues differently. We made a contract that when that happened we would both stay engaged in the therapy and work it through, even if it was difficult.

ORGANIZING THE THERAPY

It is usually a good idea to have a plan for a course of therapy that is based on the client's own goals and the therapist's recommendations. It is not something I always do formally, but in this case I believed it would be a good idea. A sudden bout of depression can feel like total regression and easily make one lose sight of progress. I wanted Roberta to have a concrete record of where she was beginning, each step she wanted to traverse, and a list of the eventual goals she wanted to reach. In so doing, I was also taking advantage of and highlighting an aspect of her adult egostate—her skills of organization and logic that had served her so well as an engineer.

Roberta seemed to know her goals. She wanted to stop feeling abused at home and at work and she wanted to be kinder to herself. We agreed on the general steps necessary to get her there: increased body awareness so she could assess the immediate effects of external

and internal abuse, changing her internal dialogue to be more supportive, and taking an assertiveness training course to gain skills and confidence to protect herself and stand her ground.

MAKING THE INNER DIALOGUE EXPLICIT

The core of Roberta's therapy involved theory from TA and technique
from gestalt therapy to illuminate and then change her relationship to
herself and others. When I introduced Roberta to the idea of talking
with herself she was very anxious. She hated herself and did not know
what she would say. I taught her the basics of TA theory, the parent
(critical and nurturing), adult, and child (natural and adapted) egostates. She grasped the principles easily, but feared the process. She
was, we discovered, actually quite scared of herself.

The first thing I suggested she do was to imagine her child part and
just talk to it. She started to cry. "I can't," she said. When I asked her
"Why not?" she cried even harder. After she calmed down she was able
to answer my question. She felt terrible about how she had been treat-
ing her inner child ("I say such mean and awful things!"). She did not
believe she could talk directly to her child egostate because it would
not be willing to listen to her. When she tried to imagine her child
part, she could not find her. Roberta supposed she was hiding in fear.

Over the next few weeks, however, she did find her child. I helped
Roberta to remember how her own mother had spoken to her when
she was young. My aim was to awaken that internalization and help her
to be able to use it as part of her own nurturing parent—to contact and
soothe her child part now. Using her mother's words and tone—e.g.,
calling herself "sweetie" in a caring tone instead of "idiot" in an angry
one—she was able to make contact with her young self and find ways

to be nicer to her. These slight changes in her inner dialogue gradually led to bigger changes. One day Roberta announced that she now saw her periodic days spent in bed as an opportunity for nurturing instead of a shameful retreat. She had started to look forward to those days, stocking up on hot cocoa and magazines. She readily agreed that actually scheduling a periodic "retreat day" would be a good way to care for herself. The more she was able to nurture her child, the more relaxed she became. Once in a while, she reported, she would realize something she was doing was actually fun.

First I had Roberta just talk to her child in her mind. After she got the hang of that, I asked her to voice the inner dialogue out loud. Later, when she became more comfortable, I instructed her to move between chairs, identifying with the egostate she was speaking from and carrying on an explicit dialogue.

IDENTIFYING THE INNER CRITIC

The most difficult work was helping Roberta to make amends with her inner critic. She so hated this part of her, the one who had hurt her all of these years, that forgiveness was incomprehensible. Luckily, though, something different happened during one session. I noticed a change in Roberta's posture while she was sitting in the critical parent chair: Instead of being the usual imposing, powerful figure, she began to shrink, visibly. Her voice also changed, rising slightly higher in pitch. I stopped Roberta to ask her what was going on in her body and in her mind. She said that she was feeling rather young: She felt like swinging her legs and was feeling restless rather than angry. I believed that there had been an important shift in egostates, so I brought in another chair and had Roberta move to it. I proceeded to interview this new egostate that had seemingly emerged from the critical parent. It turned out to be the egostate that had developed in response to the bullying at school, the adapted child. It was this child part who had learned to be so self-critical and self-taunting.

While continuing the dialogue, Roberta remembered how she had struggled to manage the changes with her peer group. This was one more thing that she did not want to burden her parents with, so she endured it alone. At 9 years old she made a decision to beat her peers to the punch by making jokes about her lack of hair, and she became the class clown. Inwardly, she called herself the same names as the taunts, and some worse. Her logic had been that if she did it first, she would have a better chance of fitting in. It also removed some of the sting. When that resolution did not help to reintegrate her into the group, she withdrew and became a loner. But the self-depreciating inner dialogue continued. Once she decided to treat herself like that, she forgot that she could *un*decide it. Goulding and Goulding (1979) suggest pinpointing such decisions, as they are often the key to unlocking the dysfunctional internal relationship. Once a decision becomes conscious, it is possible to "redecide" it.

Typical of these kinds of early defensive strategies, this one was double-edged. On the one hand it mediated a worse onslaught by her classmates. On the other hand, the decision to call herself names became habitual. As is usual under such circumstances, she soon forgot the origin of her self-criticism and continued to taunt, criticize, and hurt herself even once she was "normal" again. She also came to expect taunts and criticism from others, setting in motion the pattern that eventually led her to my office.

This session was a turning point in Roberta's therapy. For the first time she realized that her critical voice had developed in an effort to protect her, not to hurt her. In addition, it was clear that this part of her was young and insecure, whereas before she had assumed it was old and authoritative. Objectively at first, and later emotionally, Roberta came to appreciate her 9 year old's efforts to protect her. Rather than hating her, she was eventually able to forgive and even thank her adapted child for her efforts to resolve the problems she had faced. It then became possible to redecide that old decision to self-taunt and do something different. From then on Roberta began to change how she talked to her inner critic. She treated it as a hurt child, rather than as a punishing grown-up. Gradually, the adapted child and the critical parent began to soften, and the critical voice lost the power to devastate.

THERAPY REVIEW

In the course of the 2½ years that I worked with Roberta, we utilized many interventions and also spent a number of sessions just talking. The psychopharmacologist periodically adjusted her medication, once adding a small amount of stimulant for a brief period of time to help her over a difficult hump. Toward the end of her treatment, Roberta was gradually weaned from her medication.

During the last 6 months of her therapy, Roberta made many changes in her life. Once she was kinder to herself, she began to expect it from others. Her work situation was impossible to change, as her boss firmly believed that the only way to get adequate work from the staff was to criticize them. Once that became clear, Roberta found another job.

Whether or not to leave her husband was another matter. She realized that they basically did love each other. Though she was pushed to threaten separation at one point, he finally acquiesced and agreed to couples counseling. They were referred to one of my colleagues, who helped them to change their negative communication patterns.

In reviewing the therapy at the time of termination, Roberta gave me feedback on what had been most helpful. The assertiveness training course had proven to be an excellent adjunct to the therapy. Before taking it she was bereft of strategies for defending herself and getting her needs met. The course helped her to have a language for saying "yes," "no," and "stop." She had feared it would make her a "bitch," but found instead that she actually became nicer when she felt less threatened and was able to stop people from mistreating her. The most important part, however, had been learning to accept herself and talk to herself in a respectful and supportive manner. The tools from TA and gestalt, she felt, were the ones that provided the firm foundation for all of the changes she managed to make.

CHAPTER TEN

Controlling Intrusive Images

NEURO-LINGUISTIC PROGRAMMING, SOMATIC TRAUMA THERAPY

A sense of control—mastery over one's world and mind—are often casualties of trauma. That feeling of loss of control is perpetuated by the discomforting symptoms of PTSD. Often the most disturbing of these symptoms is the reexperiencing of events via intrusive images of trauma that encroach on the individual's daily life (APA, 1994). Intrusive images are rarely recognized as the memories or symbols of memories that they usually are. Instead, their intensity makes the individual feel as if the past traumatic event is happening in the here and now. Intrusive images can be triggered by internal or external cues. These images can appear in any sensory form, but visual images are the most common (or at least the most studied). The subjective experience is one of loss of control—that is, the images are in charge and come and go as they please. The individual usually feels helpless, frightened, and further victimized.

A major factor for safe trauma therapy is to put the survivor in command of her situation as much as possible. Helping her to be in charge of traumatic images is a major step in that direction. Learning that images can be controlled can be a revelation for someone suffering from PTSD. A few simple interventions can give the client a tremendous sense of control over these heretofore uncontrollable intrusions.

The following interventions are inspired by NLP's (neuro-linguistic programming) concept of *submodalities* (Andreas & Andreas, 1987; Bandler, 1985). The idea is simple, the effect profound. Submodalities are the qualities of senses: Visual submodalities, for example, include color, intensity, and size; auditory submodalities include volume and pitch; touch submodalities include pressure and temperature. In the cases discussed below, the goal is to help each client to take control of his visual images, by changing the submodalities in as many ways as possible. These cases illustrate the usefulness of this approach. The first is a session transcript; the second, is a short case description in which the technique was adapted to another circumstance. Image control is the major tool for both.

Adaptation of these concepts illustrates the "ten foundations" principle of tailoring every therapy to the client's needs. I do not think of these techniques as constituting a complete therapy method, but it is a great advantage to have such handy tools to pull out as part of the course of therapy. Readers are encouraged to digest the principles and use them when appropriate, *further adapting* them to the needs of *their* clients. This might mean, for example, focusing on changing auditory images instead of visual ones, changing somatic sensations, creating other kinds of manipulations, or slowing the process down over many sessions.

The addition of body and emotional awareness to gauge and pace the process comes from somatic trauma therapy.

JORDAN: IMAGES OF 9/11

Jordan came to me still suffering 3 months after the September 11, 2001, attacks on New York. What had once been acute stress disorder was moving steadily towards PTSD. His job was in the downtown area of a midwestern city and he had trouble driving to work. Images of the two jetliners crashing into the World Trade Center and the buildings' collapse were etched into his mind's eye. As he neared the area of downtown on his way to work each morning, he would break into a cold sweat and become nauseous. He could not stand to look up at a skyscraper. Every time he did, he saw the image of a jetliner crashing into it. So far he had coped, but each day it became harder to drive to work. Sometimes at night, the same images would intrude as he drifted into sleep, causing him to startle and delaying his sleep.

The following transcript begins 10 minutes into Jordan's third session.*

THERAPIST: Jordan, can you imagine a TV or movie screen in front of you?

JORDAN: Yes, no problem.

THERAPIST: Describe it.

JORDAN: It's like that kind they used at school when we got to have science films. It's a long metallic tube that sits on a tripod. You have to lift the screen up out of the tube and hook it on a bar above.

THERAPIST: Great. Now tell me how far away it is from you.

---

*This transcript moves much more quickly than the actual therapy, as it does not reflect the time elapsed when Jordan silently followed instructions.

JORDAN: About five feet.

THERAPIST: Can you place it farther away, say about ten feet?

JORDAN: Yes, that's easy.

THERAPIST: About how big is it?

JORDAN: Maybe four feet by six feet.

THERAPIST: Can you see that perspective?

THERAPIST: Yes.

The first goal was to establish his ability to create images. I was targeting visual images here because that was the problem he presented with. Had he presented with difficulties with intrusive auditory images, I would have focused on those, using an imagined cassette recorder or the like. It actually wasn't necessary for his images to be 100% clear; the clarity of the imagined images usually matches that of the intruding images.

THERAPIST: Good. Now I'm going to ask you to do something a bit harder. Shrink the screen by about 10%. Can you do that?

Beginning image manipulation with something neutral gave him a no-risk taste of the process.

JORDAN: Yes, no problem.

THERAPIST: Fine. Now do that again, another 10%.

JORDAN: Okay. Done.

THERAPIST: Now, what picture or vista do you like looking at?

I wanted to establish a positive image that we could revert to as an anchor if or when the going got rough.

JORDAN: That's easy, my daughter's face.

THERAPIST: Can you project her face on the screen?

JORDAN: Yes.

THERAPIST: Tell me what she looks like.

JORDAN: She has brown hair and eyes. Her eyes are really big and are looking right at me. She is smiling, big. I can see the gap between her two front teeth—she's going to the orthodontist soon to fix that.

THERAPIST: Okay, now another difficult task. See if you can change the picture to black and white. Can you do it?

Manipulating an image with positive associations is also low-risk. We were building his ability, just as you might begin learning to swim in the shallow end of the pool.

JORDAN: Yes, it's not hard.

THERAPIST: That's great. Now try making it green and white.

JORDAN: Done.

THERAPIST: Can you turn her head forty-five degrees to the right?

JORDAN: Yes.

THERAPIST: Tip her head so she is looking up?

JORDAN: Yes.

THERAPIST: Have her look straight at you again, smiling, and see if you can close the gap in her teeth to look as she will when the braces come off.

Trying something difficult with this image would help him to be more confident that he could change an upsetting image.

JORDAN: (*laughs*) I wish I could really do that—it would save me a lot of money!

THERAPIST: How are you feeling?

JORDAN: Calm and relaxed. This is sort of fun. Is it really therapy?

Adding a little humor or fun to trauma therapy can be a great benefit.

THERAPIST: I wanted to give you a low-key, positive experience of controlling visual images. You really seem to have the hang of it. How does it feel to you?

It is always a good idea to share rationale with clients, as it helps them to be a partner in the process.

JORDAN: It seems really easy.

THERAPIST: Do you think you could bring back this picture of your daughter anytime you wanted?

JORDAN: Sure, I couldn't forget her face.

Good. We successfully established an anchor. It was there to call on as needed.

THERAPIST: Then I'd like to go to the next step that will be a bit more difficult emotionally. I'll guide you in doing some of the same things with the images that have been haunting you. Do you feel ready to try?

JORDAN: Now I'm getting nervous.

THERAPIST: What is happening in your body that tells you that?

JORDAN: I can't breathe as easily, and my arms feel stiff.

THERAPIST: Okay. Put your daughter's face back on the screen. Can you do it?

JORDAN: (*exhales*) Yes. She's back.

THERAPIST: How do you feel?

JORDAN: Oh! Calmer again, more relaxed. I can breathe.

The anchor worked.

THERAPIST: Yes. I want to remind you that you can come back to your daughter's picture any time you want.

JORDAN: Okay.

THERAPIST: Ready?

JORDAN: Yes, ready.

THERAPIST: Okay, choose one of the images that bother you, but don't pick the worst one to start. Just one.

It was important to start with something that had a good chance of being manageable. The idea here was to build on success. Better to take many successful small steps than try to hurry the process with a few big steps that could result in failure.

JORDAN: I'll start with the first image I saw on television. When I first turned on the TV I saw the first tower on fire.

It is also good to give the client the choice of image when possible.

THERAPIST: Put that image on your screen. Can you make it a still image?

JORDAN: Yes, I've seen a photograph of it.

Usually a still image is less provocative than one in motion.

THERAPIST: Is it in color?

JORDAN: Yes.

THERAPIST: Make it black and white.

Again, black and white is less provocative.

JORDAN: Okay. Done.

THERAPIST: Reduce the picture by 10%.

Making it smaller helped him gain more control. Additionally, smaller images are less threatening.

JORDAN: Done.

THERAPIST: Turn it on its side ninety degrees, with the base of the tower on the right.

JORDAN: Okay.

THERAPIST: Now turn it the other way, 180 degrees so the base is on the left.

JORDAN: Done. This is easier than I thought it would be.

He was getting the hang of being able to control the images. They were his images, and I wanted him to know that.

THERAPIST: Good. Now turn the picture right-side up and reduce it by 10% more.

JORDAN: Okay. I've got it.

THERAPIST: One more thing, fade the picture to blurry, as if the developer got it wrong or the photographer moved.

JORDAN: Yes, it's blurry. This is good!

THERAPIST: How are you feeling?

JORDAN: Surprisingly good. Calm, even. I didn't think that would be possible.

He had been creating images that previously were upsetting, but discovering that he could control them was making him calm.

THERAPIST: Are you ready to try it with a moving image?

JORDAN: Yes. But I think I'll start with that picture of my daughter first.

THERAPIST: Good idea, do that.

It is always encouraging when the client realizes he can use his anchor when-ever he wants. When a client initiates the anchor, I gain confidence in present-ing him with more difficult material. This tells me he is beginning to recognize his limits.

JORDAN: Now I'm ready.

THERAPIST: Fine. Now, in addition to the screen, I want you to imagine a VCR within your reach. I mean the kind that has buttons for forward, reverse, fast forward, fast reverse, pause, slow motion, etc. A fancy one. Then choose a disturbing image that has movement in it—again, not the worst one.

JORDAN: Okay, that's when the second tower collapses.

THERAPIST: I'd like you to start with the middle of the sequence, when the tower is half collapsed. First run it backwards in 10 seconds.

Starting with the middle of the sequence was an unusual manipulation, and one that I hoped would reinforce the idea that he was in control of these images.

JORDAN: Done.

THERAPIST: Now run it forwards half way in 10 seconds. Stop when the tower is half collapsed.

JORDAN: Okay.

THERAPIST: How are you doing?

JORDAN: I'm a little anxious.

THERAPIST: How do you experience that in your body?

JORDAN: My hands have gone cold and my stomach is tight.

Signs of SNS hyperarousal. It was time to put on the brakes by bringing in the anchor.

THERAPIST: Okay, switch to the picture of your daughter's smiling face.

JORDAN: (*exhales, smiles slightly*) It is so good to be able to come back to her face.

THERAPIST: Can you feel you are breathing again?

JORDAN: Yes. I hadn't realized I'd been holding my breath.

THERAPIST: How is your hand temperature and stomach tension?

JORDAN: My hands are warmed up and my stomach is mostly normal.

Body awareness told us both that the hyperarousal had reduced and the PNS was more active. Without him saying it, we both knew he was no longer anxious.

THERAPIST: Shall we continue?

JORDAN: Yes, please.

THERAPIST: Okay. I'd like you to run that film forward and back between half collapse and full height several times, quite quickly.

JORDAN: This isn't fun like the other images, but I do have the hang of it and it's just astonishing I can do it.

THERAPIST: Do what?

Until this point I had been instructing him. Now I wanted him to name what he was doing, make a cognitive connection to his role in the process. I wanted him to make sense of the exercise and its purpose. This is a potential point for integration.

JORDAN: Control these pictures that have been controlling me for so long.

THERAPIST: How does *that* feel?

JORDAN: *That* feels fantastic.

THERAPIST: Are you ready for the harder part?

JORDAN: You mean having the tower collapse completely?

THERAPIST: Exactly, but first do it from half to full collapse back and forth several times.

JORDAN: Yes. That is easier to do than I thought. I'm ready to see it collapse from its full height.

Jordan was progressing quickly. I wouldn't expect such rapid progress with most trauma clients. However, Jordan had many resources and was quite stable prior to September 11th. This exercise reminded him of his resources; we didn't need to build them from scratch as I do with some of my clients.

THERAPIST: All right, but change the color combination—black and white, sepia, green and white, something like that.

JORDAN: I'll do it in sepia; it will remind me of the Mexican scenes in [the movie] *Traffic*.

THERAPIST: How's it going?

JORDAN: It's going okay. The strange thing of it is that I still hate seeing it, but I don't feel so devastated by it. It makes a difference that I am running the film instead of it running me.

Another cognitive integration. He was making sense both of the exercise and of the mechanism behind his previous upset. Until today he'd felt controlled by those images.

THERAPIST: I think that is a great way to put it. Are you ready to take charge of the most distressing image?

JORDAN: Yes. Of the second plane flying into the second tower. (*takes a deep breath*) I'm ready.

THERAPIST: How do you want to control this image?

JORDAN: I get to choose?

THERAPIST: Yes, I think you are ready to take full charge.

I wanted him to know he could continue this without my guidance whenever these or any other images intruded.

JORDAN: Like a final exam?

THERAPIST: I hadn't thought of it that way, but maybe that's a good analogy. What would you like to do?

JORDAN: I'd like to make the plane go very, very slowly. Part of what was so shocking was how quickly it happened. I think I also want to do it as a series of still photographs rather than a film—snap, snap, snap, snap . . .

THERAPIST: Try it.

JORDAN: (*with tears in his eyes*) It's the most horrible thing I have ever seen in my life. I hope never to see anything so horrible ever again. (*begins to cry*) I wish I could have stopped it, that I never saw it, that it never happened. I'm seeing my daughter's face now. She is so young and innocent, but that day changed the world for her, too. I am afraid for her future.

Finally, there was an emotional connection. It was likely that these thoughts and feelings, when unexpressed, were fueling the intrusive images.

THERAPIST: What are you feeling in your body?

JORDAN: I'm shaking a bit. I remember shaking that day, but trying to stop it because I felt I had to pull myself together. I wanted to be strong for my daughter, for my family. I didn't want them to be more afraid because I was.

THERAPIST: That is good to shake a bit. Just let that happen.

Shaking is often a somatic response to releasing traumatic stress. When it reduces arousal, it is a good idea to just let it happen (Levine, 1997). Had

Jordan not stopped himself from shaking on that traumatic day, the long-range traumatic impact may not have been so great.

THERAPIST: (*after the shaking subsides*) Go back to the image of the plane.

JORDAN: It's not as easy to see now. There's a bit of fog between me and it.

A good sign that he was distancing from the trauma. This effect is also often seen with EMDR, which also works to reduce the impact of traumatic imagery.

THERAPIST: That's just fine. The fog may get thicker or thinner. Actually, you can change it yourself, but I'd just leave it for now. How are you feeling?

JORDAN: Sad. And very tired.

THERAPIST: Okay, one last task. I want you to imagine driving to work tomorrow, nearing downtown, seeing the skyscrapers. How do you feel?

JORDAN: I'm not scared, but I still feel sad. I also feel very grateful as I look up at the skyline that our city is whole. We were lucky.

Further cognitive integration.

THERAPIST: It's possible that the intrusive images could appear again. What would you do?

Because his problem had permeated his daily life, it was important to antici-pate that it could persist. Planning for future intrusions would make it possible for him to be able to continue to feel in control.

JORDAN: Well, I have a lot of choices to try. First, I'd probably rather see my daughter's face. But it might be a good idea to change the image, turn the plane back, for example. They are just images, I can do what I want with them!

This was the integration I had hoped for. If he could hang on to that truth, the images would no longer bother him.

THERAPIST: I think this is a good place to stop. I suggest you take a bit of a walk before you drive home. Let this settle. You've worked very hard.

This session proceeded very neatly. It was easy and uncomplicated. As mentioned, this was in large part because Jordan came to the session already highly resourced. As many clients have fewer resources, it is important that readers not try to apply these interventions exactly as illustrated. Sometimes clients complain that the negative images are still intruding, or that they are not able to change an image. When that happens, it is important to slow things down and backtrack. Go back to an image or a manipulation that the client *can* do without negative intrusion and then go slowly forward from there. The important thing is to build on positive, successful experiences. Each client's need for repetition will be different, but the eventual goal is for the client, as Jordan did here, to realize that he is controlling his images.

It can be tempting to allow clients to manipulate images like this in complete silence, focusing on implicit processes. I would not, however, recommend that. Language is necessary for accessing explicit memory and cognitive processing. For integration to take place, the client must be able to make verbal sense of what has and is happening.

BRENNAN: ANGRY EYES

Brennan's trauma therapy got stuck when images of a sadistic teacher's angry eyes continued to intrude. Regardless of the intervention, he was unable to free himself of this look.

Brennan and I had developed a good relationship, and I was fairly confident that he perceived me as an ally. So I thought it was worth trying something different. I asked him to look at my eyes and commit them to memory: their color, shape, placement, expression. (I also could have used the image of the eyes of a friend or someone else he felt safe with.) He was able to do this easily, as he was used to looking at me for an hour or more each week.

The next thing I suggested was for him to look away from me, at the wall or out of the window, and call up the memory of my eyes. This was not hard for him to do; if it had been, I would have asked him to look back at me and away again repeatedly until he could take the image of my eyes with him.

When Brennan could hold the image of my eyes in his mind's eye, I suggested ways in which he could change my eyes—color, shape, expression, etc.—one item at a time. We actually did this over several sessions, and I gave him assignments for homework.

Once he became adept at manipulating the remembered image of my eyes, I suggested he try it with the teacher's eyes. First I had him place them at various distances. Then he went on to experiment with changing their color, shape, and expression. Again, we did this in small bits over many sessions. He even took it upon himself to draw the teacher's eyes and use crayons to make changes.

Eventually Brennan became capable of image manipulation and realized that he controlled the memory of his teacher's eyes. At a subsequent therapy session, when I asked how it was going, Brennan suddenly realized that the images had not intruded for several days. He was astonished and we celebrated his newfound freedom. Addressing the traumas associated with that teacher became easier after that.

CHAPTER ELEVEN

Back in the Family

PSYCHODYNAMIC PSYCHOTHERAPY, ATTACHMENT THEORY

Childhood sexual abuse can cause the child to become isolated from his family even when the perpetrator is someone outside of the family. In the following case example, psychodynamic psychotherapy and application of attachment theory are major tools in helping the client to understand his isolation, and to help him back into the fold of his family.

When Terry was 13 years old he was molested by a 17-year-old stranger who had been visiting a neighborhood friend. The older boy had coerced Terry into a situation where they were alone and then molested him. Terry was intimidated into acquiescence by the teen's size and strength and by the threat that if Terry squealed or didn't comply, he would be killed. Terry had watched enough television to believe the boy's threats. He desperately wanted to confide in his parents, but the fear of reprisal was too great. He was never able to tell them.

He finally dared reveal his secret to his first gay lover when he was 18. Unfortunately, that young man was aroused rather than horrified when he heard about the incident, and Terry felt more alone and humiliated than ever.

Now in his early twenties, Terry sought therapy because he was socially isolated and unable to enjoy sex with either men or women. Whenever he became aroused, visual images of the molestation intruded, and the threat of death echoed in his ears. He felt ashamed, dirty, frightened, angry, and out of control.

Until age 13, Terry's childhood experiences had been mostly positive. His family was cohesive, and, the oldest of four, he was relatively close to his younger siblings. His parents were, for the most part, available, loving, and supportive, if a bit overwhelmed by meeting the needs and extracurricular schedules of four children.

A major consequence of the molestation was that Terry felt very distanced from his family. He withdrew and became a loner. The solace he had usually found in his family became inaccessible. Both his mother and father sensed something was wrong and tried to get him to talk. However, they were unable to pierce the fear that kept Terry's secret bound—he knew if he told his parents, they would call the police, and the molester would follow through on his threat. Terry's parents eventually concluded that his personality change was due to puberty— some of their friend's adolescents had also suddenly stopped talking to their parents—and dealt with him from that perspective. With three younger children, Terry's parents had plenty to keep them occupied. They did not exactly give up on Terry, but they lacked the time and energy to be persistent.

In the years since the molestation Terry kept contact with his parents and siblings, mostly by attending family gatherings. But the relationships were strained and he often felt more like an outsider than a member of the family. Though his family accepted that he was gay, he still felt like the odd man out.

Terry fit well into the trauma type IIB(R). Prior to age 13, he was well-resourced and early bonding was strong. Terry had many resources to be reawakened or reassociated, which was an advantage.

Attachment was an obvious issue. Terry's early life included a strong attachment to both parents and siblings. The trauma of molestation changed that. Further, his one attempt at telling a lover went terribly wrong. All told, the relationship between Terry and his therapist would be especially important, particularly his perception of how the therapist responded to being told about the molestation.

The following overview summarizes therapy sessions that took place over a 9-month period. I used psychodynamic psychotherapy to help Terry to consider the impact of the molestation on his current life. Application of attachment theory allowed me to use the therapeutic relationship as a rehearsal ground where Terry could try out new behaviors and then gradually expand his contact to others, especially his family. As was the case here, the therapist can become a teacher or coach in helping the client master the practical side of interpersonal communication—to teach him, in this case, how to talk to others about his deepest feelings.

THERAPY, MONTHS 1–2: ESTABLISHING RELATIONSHIPS

At first Terry wanted to brush his feelings aside. He discounted my empathy, claiming that I was a "professional" and had to respond with concern. It was difficult for him to see me as person in a professional capacity—all he could see was the profession. But, he admitted, it was the first time he had told his story without feeling further humiliated. Building on that, I encouraged him to consider if there was anyone else he might be able to tell—someone who would not be sexually interested in the story. Reluctantly he admitted he had a platonic female friend who had confided some of her own past. Terry considered whether he could share this incident with her.

It is not uncommon for those who are unused to confiding in others to be naïve about how to approach emotionally vulnerable topics. Out of anxiety, they often will take the first opportunity to blurt out what is on their mind, without considering timing or context. That can be a set-up for failure, making it harder to try again. I always try to help my clients to maximize the possibility of success in their fledgling ventures. I want them to have the best chance of getting the response they need and, with it, the positive reinforcement and encouragement to dare again. Success builds courage to persevere.

I suggested that Terry first imagine how telling his friend might go, helping him to anticipate as many contingencies as he could think of— all the things that possibly could go wrong if he told her. We also discussed how he might "stack the deck in his favor" in terms of when he told her about it—how to make sure she was in a mental and emotional mood to be able to hear him.

Eventually, Terry decided to ask his friend over for dinner, as they often liked to make pasta together. He thought it would be easier to talk at home than in a restaurant. He would wait until they'd had a glass of wine and then, if it seemed she was in a fairly good mood, he would proceed. We discussed how he could prepare his friend to hear his story, as he was afraid of scaring or overwhelming her.

Terry was pretty sure it wouldn't be a problem for his friend, but he thought that beginning with a preamble would be useful for both of them. He didn't want to jump in with both feet, or without looking. He rehearsed a couple of scenarios in his head.

By the time the evening of the dinner arrived he felt both mentally and emotionally ready. The preparation we had done together helped him to perceive me as an ally—a coconspirator, as it were. We also arranged that he could call me the next day if something went awry and he needed the support. In any event, we had an appointment scheduled for the next week.

He didn't call. When he arrived on time for his next session he was calmer than I had ever seen him. He told me about the evening with his friend and how he had slowly approached telling her about being molested. It had gone well. She had been interested, but not intrusive; concerned, but not motherly. Terry finally felt that someone whom he felt close to—a friend, not a therapist—had listened to what had happened and cared. His friend was also able to grasp the enormous impact the event had had on Terry's life, and he was able to cry a little when she hugged him in consolation. For the first time in nearly 10 years, he no longer felt alone.

At this point, a couple of months into his therapy, Terry and I discussed applying other tools that might be useful in helping him resolve the molestation and other issues. None of the trauma therapies I had to offer (outlined elsewhere in this book) appealed to him. He had hesitated to engage in therapy in the first place because he hated the idea of techniques. No, he was quite content to talk with me, even if that took a little longer. No matter what I thought might work more quickly, respecting his wishes was crucial.

THERAPY, MONTHS 3–5:
INTRUSION OF THE PAST ON THE PRESENT

During these months, Terry's therapy focused on how past events, both positive and negative, affected his life today. Of course, much of the discussion focused on the difficulties that had developed since the molestation and how the consequences of that had permeated his life. Increasingly, though, it also became important to help Terry to remember and recognize the resources he had developed in his first 13 years, when life was easier and he felt more supported. The question that became most relevant was: Who is Terry today and how is he a culmination of *all* of his experiences, not just of the traumatic one that stands out?

THERAPY, MONTHS 6–7:
FAMILY RELATIONSHIPS, THEN AND NOW

Terry had a lot of mourning to do. One of the worst consequences of the molestation was that he lost his feeling of family ties. He had missed feeling close to his family more than he had dared to let himself know.

He made contacts with his younger siblings, spending more time with those who lived nearby. With a lot of preparation, Terry finally told the brother he was closest to about the molestation. Rather than judging him, as Terry had feared, his brother was grateful to be told. He had always known something had happened, he just hadn't known what. He had also missed Terry terribly when the closeness they had disappeared. He'd been angry at Terry's distance and had acted that out in the kinds of vengeful ways children do. He apologized for any additional hurt he had caused his older brother.

With that success under his belt, Terry attempted to get closer to his youngest sister, who was now a teenager. Unfortunately, she wasn't interested. There were too many years between them for her to have felt very close to him as a child. Terry believed she had a chip on her shoulder and felt hurt. We discussed the pros and cons of persisting at this time, and Terry decided it would be better to back off. He'd had enough success at this point that he wasn't deterred by her rejection. He also speculated that when she got older, she might come around. Remembering the trials of adolescence—not so long ago for him either—helped him feel compassion rather than resentment toward her.

THERAPY, MONTHS 8–9:
RETURN TO THE FAMILY AND TERMINATION

Terry knew the next step. He wanted to find a way to finally tell his parents about the molestation. His feelings were mixed and strong. On the one hand he couldn't wait, but on the other, he dreaded it. He knew his parents would be greatly upset and he knew the knowledge would hurt them. They would be enraged at what the older boy had done. They would be sad about how much it had injured Terry. But he knew it would hurt them most to realize that he had not been able to tell them at the time, and that they had not figured it out. For that they were certain to feel very guilty, and Terry was reluctant to burden his parents with that.

I encouraged him to talk this over with the woman he had first told about the molestation. She'd had some experience with talking to her own parents about difficulties. She proved to be instrumental in supporting him without pushing him. We agreed he was lucky to have such a friend. He also discussed it with his brother and gained his support. The brother would sit in with Terry when he told his parents.

Terry decided he wanted to have adequate time to address the issue. He didn't want to tell them and then disappear. So he planned to travel home to visit over a long weekend. He prepared his parents by telling them he had something important he wanted to discuss with them, but didn't tell them what it was. He arranged with his friend that she would be at her own home most of that weekend so that he could call her for coaching and moral support if he needed it. His brother also would be there. Of course, he knew that he could call me, but I would be more difficult to reach.

After the weekend with his parents, Terry came to therapy to report his success, but also to complain of depression, which scared him. He had been tired, sad, and listless since he had returned. It quickly became clear that he was having a grief reaction, something I should have anticipated. Regaining contact with most of his siblings, and especially with his parents, opened the floodgates for him to finally feel what he had lost and missed over the last 10 years. Over the next weeks, both in and out of therapy, Terry cried a lot.

Once his grief waned, Terry felt ready to terminate therapy. He didn't think of termination as an attempt to go it alone. On the contrary, he found that he now had more support than he had ever expected, and that therapy had become an adjunct rather than a central source. At our last meeting he thanked me for helping him back to his family.

CHAPTER TWELVE

Job Loss and Public Shame

COGNITIVE BEHAVIORAL THERAPY, SOMATIC TRAUMA THERAPY

The emotion of shame and the issue of self-forgiveness, although often neglected, are central in working with trauma. Technically, being laid off or fired is not a trauma, as it doesn't pose an actual threat to life—there is no weapon, no physical injury. However, when job loss threatens one's livelihood, it can be perceived as a threat to life, and, the internal response can be very similar to traumatic stress.

Iris was 61 years old. She was not financially or emotionally ready to retire, nor was she yet eligible for social security. She had worked for many years as a secretary in a large corporation. Competent in her job, at the highest salary for her employment level, she had never aspired to move further upward. For a long time she had been very comfortable and felt secure. She planned to retire in 4 years when her company pension and social security would make it affordable. All went well until a new department manager was hired and Iris suddenly had a new supervisor. They did not get along. Iris felt the supervisor had her targeted. Mostly she was able to skirt around the supervisor and just do her work. But eventually conflict became unavoidable. One day, without warning, Iris was publicly humiliated, laid off, and made to leave the office within a matter of minutes.

For the 3 months following the dismissal, Iris suffered panic attacks and cried almost daily. She was too nervous and too ashamed to look for a new job, and she felt hopeless about finding anything "at my age" anyway. She had not even filed for unemployment. Friends had urged her to seek legal advice, but it was all too overwhelming for Iris. At the urging of her granddaughter, she sought psychological help.

Our first sessions helped Iris to contain her wealth of emotion and hyperarousal. Body awareness and muscle toning were particularly useful for her. Between sessions she had ample opportunity to use those new tools, as she was often aroused. I asked Iris to keep a log noting which situations and thoughts triggered her arousal. Additionally, I encouraged her to tend to her garden—much neglected since she was laid off—as it had always been a source of comfort and an engaging activity. Over a period of a few weeks, her frayed nerves began to settle as she identified triggers and decreased their impact. Less anxious and more in control, Iris began to feel angry, a healthy sign. Rather than discharging the anger, I helped Iris to become comfortable with it and to use it to her advantage. It gave her increased energy to take direct action and helped her to feel less vulnerable.

The next steps were practical. Aided by her newfound anger and with the assistance of her granddaughter, Iris applied for unemployment, engaged a lawyer, and began to search the want ads for secretarial jobs. Those processes underway, Iris felt better and was ready to address the events and emotions of that horrible day she was laid off.

When Iris first came to therapy, she was much too overwhelmed and unstable to address the events surrounding her layoff. Had we attempted to do that in the beginning, the risk of further decompensation and becoming overwhelmed would have been great. But with her stabilized, stronger, and less vulnerable, it was safe to proceed. In addition, through our preparatory work, Iris had developed body awareness as a useful resource and we had established a good working relationship.

THERAPIST: How is this distance between us?

IRIS: I would like for you to come closer to me.

THERAPIST: Okay, about how much?

IRIS: One foot.

THERAPIST: Here?

IRIS: Yes. A little bit back, please.

THERAPIST: Okay.

IRIS: Okay that's fine.

THERAPIST: How do you know?

IRIS: I can feel it.

THERAPIST: Where?

IRIS: In my chest. I'm relaxing, can breathe easier.

THERAPIST: So you were tense in your chest and I moved back and now you're relaxed?

IRIS: Yes. Maybe I would like to be like this so we aren't facing each other so directly (*turns her chair slightly to the left*).

THERAPIST: That's fine. I'm glad you are being precise. How's this now?

IRIS: It's okay, feels fine.

THERAPIST: Before we look at what happened at work, I want to make sure there is something we can use to change the subject that feels good to talk about. What would work for you?

We were establishing an anchor that could be used to put on the brakes when she became hyperaroused.

IRIS: That could either be my garden or my granddaughter (*she smiles*).

THERAPIST: Talk about each one in turn for a minute or so and see which feels the most comfortable in your body and helps you to feel the most calm.

IRIS: (*She talks at length about them one at a time.*)

THERAPIST: Which feels most relaxing to you?

IRIS: It is a bit hard to say. When I talk about my garden I feel very relaxed. I can smell the earth and flowers and my breathing is easy. When I talk about my granddaughter I smile and feel warm, proud, and cared for. I don't know which to choose.

THERAPIST: Does your granddaughter ever visit you in your garden, or ever help you with your work there?

IRIS: Why, yes. When she was a child, she used to come and help me a lot in the summers. I gave her her own patch where she could grow vegetables—you know, the kind children like: carrots, radishes, strawberries. Since college though, she never has as much time. But she sometimes comes on the weekends and helps me. Then we chat over lunch or tea. I love those days.

THERAPIST: How would that be for a solution, then? To take breaks talking about your granddaughter working in the garden with you?

IRIS: I like that idea. That would be fine.

THERAPIST: So, are you ready to talk about work?

IRIS: (*paling slightly*) Oh, I guess so.

THERAPIST: Can you feel that something just changed?

IRIS: Yes, I'm starting to get nervous. It has been so nice to not talk much about work for a few weeks. I guess I am a bit worried to stir it all up.

THERAPIST: What would help you to have more courage to face it?

IRIS: (*takes a big breath*) If I knew I could get out from under it again, that I could control my crying and the panic attacks.

THERAPIST: That's actually why I wanted to find something to talk about that was pleasant and calming for you. That's called an anchor. When talking about work gets difficult, when you get very anxious or uneasy, we'll stop talking about that and talk about your granddaughter visiting you in your garden instead. That way you can learn to go into and then come out of the difficult feelings at will. The memories of your garden and your granddaughter will be the anchor to pull you out of emotional difficulty.

IRIS: Oh! That sounds like a very good idea.

THERAPIST: How are you feeling right now?

IRIS: Calmer again.

THERAPIST: And, I forgot to mention, we will take it slowly. Okay?

IRIS: Okay. Then how do we start?

THERAPIST: Can you give me an overview of what happened the day you were laid off?

As can be seen from the first part of this session, Iris now had an easy control of her arousal. At this point I planned to just let her talk about that day and see what emerged as a pressing issue. I wouldn't be so loose with every client, but Iris had adjusted well, been able to use just about every tool I sent her way, and had many internal and external resources. I wasn't worried about anything getting out of hand.

IRIS: I don't know if I remember it all correctly. Everything happened so fast. My new supervisor, Melinda, she just came up to me in the middle of the secretarial pool and said really loud, "Gather your things, Iris, you'll be leaving us today." She didn't even say "good morning," "hello," or give any kind of preamble. For a minute I just sat there, dumbfounded. (*She speeds up her tempo.*) Then I started to ask her what was going on. She . . .

Iris began to cry, a panicked kind of crying with an emphasis on the inhale. This kind of crying increases hyperarousal, so I call it "sympathetic crying." It is not a release—it actually creates more distress—so I always put on the brakes when it occurs.

THERAPIST: Hold on a just a minute. I'm going to stop you from crying like that. Say some words, tell me what is happening inside.

IRIS: (*slows down, catches her breath*) I was starting to panic, remembering how shocked I was. I didn't know what was going on. It all happened so fast.

THERAPIST: What is happening in your body?

IRIS: I can feel I'm shaking and my hands are cold.

THERAPIST: So let's use your anchor. When is the last time your daughter came to visit you in your garden?

IRIS: A couple of weeks ago. She came on Saturday morning and helped me plant a bed of herbs. She lives nearby and I told her to come and get whatever she wanted anytime.

THERAPIST: Did you have lunch that day?

IRIS: Oh, yes. Let me see. I made her favorite, my special chicken salad. She likes it just like I do, with celery and green grapes.

THERAPIST: How are you feeling right now?

IRIS: Much better.

THERAPIST: How?

IRIS: My hands are warming up and I've stopped shaking.

THERAPIST: What happened to the panic?

IRIS: Oh! You are right. That went away completely. I didn't know it could be stopped. Thank you!

THERAPIST: How did *you* stop it?

I wanted Iris to know she now had tools to reduce her panic herself—that it was not just some type of magic that only I could do.

IRIS: By slowing my crying and by talking about my granddaughter and garden. That really worked!

THERAPIST: So what do you think about going on?

IRIS: Yes, that's fine. So Melinda is just standing there waiting for me to move. But I wanted to know what was going on and said so. She just kept repeating that I must gather my personal things and go with her. Everyone else had stopped working and was staring at us. I didn't want to go. I wanted to stay. But I was also very embarrassed. I had no idea what I had done to deserve that kind of treatment.

THERAPIST: How many people were there?

IRIS: Well it's a big room, probably about twenty were in easy earshot. More could see Melinda standing over me.

THERAPIST: How do you feel right now in your body as you talk about this?

IRIS: I can feel my heart beat quickly. And I'm a little dizzy. My hands are cold again.

THERAPIST: Let's move back to your anchor. Which herbs did you plant with your granddaughter?

Though more contained, Iris's arousal was still pretty high. I find that it is better to use an anchor liberally in the beginning. Once clients have confidence that they can come out of feeling overwhelmed and upset, they often don't need it as much.

IRIS: Let me see . . . basil, lemon thyme, parsley, rosemary, and oregano. Next time she comes we are going to add sage and cilantro.

THERAPIST: What are your favorites?

IRIS: Mine are thyme and oregano; hers are basil and rosemary.

THERAPIST: Can you remember how they smell? Try each.

IRIS: I can! Some of them, anyway.

THERAPIST: How are you feeling in your body?

IRIS: Oh, calmed down again. That's pretty clever, your anchor idea. Shall I go on?

Now she was really showing courage, to volunteer to go back to addressing the traumatic event.

THERAPIST: Sure.

IRIS: Melinda kept insisting and was getting impatient, so I finally just went with her. I was also beginning to feel really ashamed and wanted to get away from the eyes of everyone. She took me to a cubicle, not totally private, and told me that I was laid off–just like that, can you imagine!? She told me I was to leave immediately. She made me sign some papers, telling me that if I didn't cooperate, they would fire me and I wouldn't be eligible for unemployment.

THERAPIST: So what did you do?

IRIS: I'm sorry to say, I signed the papers. I didn't have time to think about what I was doing, or the consequences, or even if they had a right to do what they were doing. She pressured me and I caved in. That's one of the hardest things of all, that I caved in. (*She dropped her head, turning it away from me.*)

THERAPIST: I see you moving your head. Tell me what is happening.

IRIS: (*sighs*) I am feeling very ashamed. I should have protested more.

THERAPIST: Are you feeling shame like you felt that day?

IRIS: Yes.

THERAPIST: What does the shame feel like in your body?

IRIS: I can't look at you, and my face is very hot.

THERAPIST: Do you know why you feel so ashamed?

IRIS: I feel like I betrayed myself because I caved in.

THERAPIST: Is that the only way to look at it?

I wanted Iris to begin to think clearly. Her level of arousal was low enough to be able to do so, even though she was feeling ashamed. Clear thinking, I believed, was going to help her resolve the issue of self-betrayal and help her to forgive her actions on that day.

IRIS: Well, no. I must have believed I'd be better off if I signed the papers and cooperated.

THERAPIST: What else could you think based on the information Melinda gave you?

IRIS: Nothing, really. But I didn't save my job.

THERAPIST: Was that even an option?

Again, I wanted her to think clearly here.

IRIS: Well, maybe not. It seems like the die was cast, all the decisions had been made before Melinda appeared at my desk. I *did* protest, but she wouldn't give an inch.

THERAPIST: You know, it is not always a good idea to judge your effort based on the outcome of a situation.

I wanted Iris to look at the situation from a different angle, not to assume there was only one cause and effect.

IRIS: I did what I could, I didn't know what else to do. It all happened so fast!

She began crying again. This time the crying was deep, with long exhales. It released her arousal, decreasing it. Her breathing became deeper and slower. This is what I refer to as "parasympathetic crying." It is calming rather than distressing. I let the crying continue until it ran its course.

THERAPIST: (*after the sobs subsided*) Do you know why you've been crying?

IRIS: I was just so confused and scared. And I felt very alone. No one made any effort to help. It was all on me. And I feel very bad that I couldn't do anything to save my job myself.

THERAPIST: What makes you think you should have been able to?

I wanted Iris to think about what happened and evaluate fairly if her expectations were fair.

IRIS: I'd been working there a long time. I believed I had good relationships with everyone except Melinda. I knew all of the ins and outs of that office, or so I thought.

THERAPIST: What was different in this situation?

IRIS: Everything! I'd never seen anyone treated like Melinda treated me. When someone was fired, it always came after a time of trying to work with the person, probation and all that. No one had ever been asked to leave on just a minute's notice before. I was stunned. Everyone was, I could see it on their faces when I dared to look at them.

THERAPIST: What do you feel in your body when you remember the image of their faces?

IRIS: Then? I felt as stunned as they did, paralyzed. Now? Well, now I feel resigned, sort of weak. I wish someone would have protested, but I can see they were all as immobile as I was.

THERAPIST: So these circumstances were very different?

IRIS: Yes. Totally.

THERAPIST: Is it possible you did your best under the circumstances, even though you couldn't stop it?

I was introducing the idea of self-forgiveness.

IRIS: How can it be my best if I didn't save my job?

THERAPIST: Your best is all you can do, though sometimes it's not enough.

IRIS: (*sighs deeply, sadly*) Yes, I can see what you mean.

THERAPIST: Do you know why your best cannot always be enough?

IRIS: I think so.

THERAPIST: Why?

IRIS: Because I can't control other people. I couldn't control the decisions that were made behind my back, and I certainly couldn't control Melinda.

THERAPIST: Yes. Just because you couldn't change their behavior, make them keep you on, doesn't mean you didn't do your best.

IRIS: Maybe I did do my best . . . (*cries, more softly this time*).

THERAPIST: (*when the crying has stopped*) Have you ever had an accident in your car that wasn't your fault?

IRIS: Yes. A few years ago. I was hit from behind.

THERAPIST: You were driving just fine just as you are supposed to do, following the rules and somebody hit you?

IRIS: Actually, I was stopped at a red light. I'd been driving for more than 40 years and I never had an accident before.

THERAPIST: You were doing your best?

IRIS: I was doing my best. Yes.

THERAPIST: Do you know why I'm asking these questions?

This is one of my favorite questions to use to help a client to think. If she didn't know the answer, though, I would tell her.

IRIS: Because it was clear that I did my best even if there was damage to my car. You're trying to connect it to my getting laid off. Making me understand I can do my best and still get hurt.

THERAPIST: Exactly. You couldn't stop the driver behind you from hitting you . . .

IRIS: . . . And I couldn't stop Melinda from laying me off.

THERAPIST: Say that again and see what happens in your body.

IRIS: (*She repeats the sentence*.) Less anxious, more relaxed, and I can feel the heat in my head reducing. I felt so ashamed, so ashamed that I just signed the papers. That was the worst thing, the shame.

Notice the spontaneous change in verb tense. She was no longer talking about feeling ashamed now, but had placed it in the past with the traumatic memory.

THERAPIST: Something just changed in your face. What's happening?

IRIS: I'm feeling somewhat relieved.

THERAPIST: How are you feeling towards yourself?

IRIS: Softer, more understanding. I don't like how it all turned out, but I can see that I really did do my best. I was trapped and there wasn't much choice.

THERAPIST: You know, actually, it's not over yet.

IRIS: Yes, I hadn't thought about that before, but you are right. There's my new lawyer. I guess it is up to her to take some action.

THERAPIST: I think it is great you were able to hire one. That wasn't easy for you.

IRIS: I guess that is part of doing my best.

THERAPIST: I agree. I think this is a good place to stop for now.

IRIS: Okay.

In subsequent sessions Iris addressed additional aspects of the layoff's emotional aftermath. Within a few months she had found another secretarial job with a smaller business, though at a slightly lower salary. Because Melinda had made such a public display of the layoff, there were many witnesses to her insensitive and abusive display. Iris's lawyer was able to negotiate a generous settlement. Iris and her granddaughter continue to work together in the garden.

CHAPTER THIRTEEN

Running to a Safe Place

BODYNAMIC RUNNING TECHNIQUE, ATTACHMENT THEORY

Usually the first step of the bodynamic running technique protocol (Jørgensen, 1992) is the recall of a safe place and a comforting person from the client's current and/or earlier life. During trauma sessions, the client imagines running to the safe place and person. The idea is to lend an imprint of support—something usually lacking during the trauma and its aftermath—to the horrifying memory of trauma. Sometimes just the reawakening of these resources is therapeutic in itself and can be used with clients who are too fragile to be candidates for the bodynamic running technique as the trauma therapy method.

It is best to stick to both a place and a person that the client has really known, so that the actual sensory memories (images, smells, sensations, etc.) can be identified. This makes the person and place easier to access in imagination. Some practitioners utilize made-up or fantasy safe places, but this eliminates the possibility (and power) of reawakening forgotten resources. Clients who cannot recall a "good enough" safe place and comforting person probably are not candidates for this method.

Hope was a 50-year-old widow, mother of three, grandmother of two. Her husband had died tragically and traumatically the year before. Hope had a hard time coming to terms with his death. She had been feeling in danger since then, and her daily functioning had suffered. Therapy had helped her function better on a day-to-day basis, but the underlying feeling of being in danger persisted. She was much too unstable at this point to use the bodynamic running technique in its entirety, but we both agreed that having a feeling of being able to run to a safe place and safe person could be of benefit to her. The following transcript is from a session that took place several weeks into her course of therapy.

THERAPIST: We agreed to set up a safe place today. Have you thought of one?

HOPE: Yes.

THERAPIST: Okay, how are you feeling right now as we start this?

HOPE: Nervous.

THERAPIST: How does your body tell you that?

HOPE: My heart is beating fast and I feel a bit tearful.

THERAPIST: Do you know what that is about?

HOPE: Fear.

THERAPIST: Fear? What are you afraid might happen?

HOPE: I'll be exposed and feel humiliated. I won't be able to handle it, I'll keep crying. I'm already starting to hyperventilate.

THERAPIST: Is that common for you to hyperventilate?

HOPE: Sort of, when I'm under stress.

THERAPIST: So you feel under stress now?

HOPE: Yes, and sad. I woke up sad, thinking about my husband. (*Her eyes become red and moist.*)

THERAPIST: As you say that, something changes. Are you hyperventilating right now?

HOPE: No.

THERAPIST: But you're more teary, aren't you?

HOPE: Yes.

THERAPIST: It looks like you stop hyperventilating when you become sad, do you feel it?

HOPE: Yes, I'm more calm.

It is quite common for anxious people to calm when they become sad. I've never seen anyone hyperventilate when they were sad.

THERAPIST: How does it feel in your chest?

HOPE: It feels better.

THERAPIST: Do you have any words for the sadness?

HOPE: It has to do with feeling alone.

THERAPIST: So do you think this might be helpful, to set up a safe place for you to run to?

HOPE: Yes. I think it might be a powerful experience.

THERAPIST: Powerful positive or powerful negative?

I just wanted to check, to make sure she saw what we had planned as potentially useful.

HOPE: Positive.

THERAPIST: How's your chest?

HOPE: I'm holding my breath, but my heart is not fast. It's okay.

THERAPIST: How's the temperature in your toes and fingers?

HOPE: Fingers are cool, but that's usual for me.

I wanted to assess her level of SNS arousal. It had lowered, so it was okay to go forward.

THERAPIST: Let's start with this and see how it goes. Your skin tone looks fine. (*Her coloring is normal, not pale.*) What is the safe place you had in mind?

HOPE: A spot in the woods by a stream. I liked to go there as a teenager.

THERAPIST: How are you feeling right now as you describe it?

HOPE: I feel calmer.

THERAPIST: What did you do there?

HOPE: I liked to sit on the shore and watch the fish, and think.

THERAPIST: What's happening in your body?

HOPE: It's just really peaceful.

Her body awareness tells us that the safe place works well.

THERAPIST: How far is it from where we are now?

HOPE: It was only about a mile from my teenage home. From here it is several hundred miles.

THERAPIST: All right, before we have you imagine running there, I'd like you to actually draw a map of how to get there from here.

When using the safe place exercise alone, as with Hope, I have the client imagine running to the safe place from my office. (A later chapter illustrates how to help a client to map and run away from the scene of a trauma.) There are several reasons behind having the client actually draw the route. First, the drawing helps crystalize the route to safety in the client's mind. Second, it makes it possible for the therapist to either follow along or direct the client along the route. Third, it gives the client something concrete to take home (if she wants) that illustrates how she was able to get away from the trauma and to the safe place. Last, the act of drawing assists in reinforcing the dual awareness of then and now: "I am drawing a picture of something that happened then."

THERAPIST: There will be two parts to the drawing: One part will be the route running away *from* here; the other part will be the route running *to* there. In between you will have to invent something to fill the gap. I don't want you running for hundreds of miles!

Jørgensen (1992, 1993) recommends a detailed image for the running. This requires specifying the first and last parts. If it is a short distance, this not difficult. But if it is far away, you need a way to collapse the distance by creating a link to the parts, a bridge. This can be provided by the image of a train, plane, magic carpet, or even a big leap.

HOPE: (*with paper and pen*) I don't know how to start.

THERAPIST: First draw where you want to land near the stream, a few hundred feet to as much as a mile away—enough so you get a feeling of running *to* it.

HOPE: Okay. I'm drawing it backwards, though.

THERAPIST: That's fine.

HOPE: All right, I did it.

THERAPIST:: Now draw the route from here, about the same distance.

HOPE: Okay.

THERAPIST: So now you need to think about how you're going to get across the gap—take a jump? run along a train? run in a Fred Flintstone car? Maybe you can think of something I haven't mentioned.

HOPE: Can I fly? On a magic carpet? I'd like that.

Many people like to imagine a magic carpet for this purpose. They can really use anything, as long as they can imagine that they keep moving. No sitting down and having a cup of coffee! The idea is to stimulate the flight reflex, so you don't want to interrupt the run.

THERAPIST: You can run onto the magic carpet, keep running along it, and then get off again by the stream. How will you get out of here?

HOPE: I'll go out that door and down the street.

THERAPIST: So you run out this door, down the walk, turn left, and run down this street?

HOPE: Yes. I get to Maple Street and run across the crosswalk.

THERAPIST: Please write the name of the street so I can guide you properly. And when you imagine running, make sure you imagine the traffic lights as being green, so you don't have to stop and wait for them.

It is important to remember that the fantasy is fully controlled by the client.

HOPE: There are small traffic lights and there's a little bridge here. Then I go across here to this road.

THERAPIST: Good. That's far enough for getting away. Then you run-jump onto the magic carpet and you land . . . where will you land?

HOPE: By a big oak that is here (*points to the drawing*). It's just outside the yard of my childhood home. I often ran to the stream from here. Along this path I come to the fence that was the boundary of our property.

THERAPIST: Over the fence or through the fence?

HOPE: Over the fence. I climb over the fence and then down the path to the stream.

THERAPIST: When you imagine running from here and to the stream, which do you think will be more comfortable, me directing you or you directing yourself?

HOPE: I don't know.

I always like to give the client the choice. Some know emphatically one way or the other. When they don't, we experiment.

THERAPIST: Then let me try it first. We can always change it.

HOPE: Okay.

THERAPIST: Let me review your route: You run out of here and down the walk. You turn left running down the street, through the green traffic lights, under the bridge, up to the next light and across that street. Then you jump on the magic carpet, run along it, and then jump off at the oak. You run down the path and climb over the fence and continue down the path to the stream. How does that sound?

HOPE: Sounds right.

THERAPIST: How are you feeling in your chest?

HOPE: I'm fine, but my mouth is a bit dry.

Some sympathetic arousal, so I checked further.

THERAPIST: And your toes and your fingers?

HOPE: Cool.

More symptoms of slight sympathetic arousal.

THERAPIST: What are you feeling right now?

HOPE: I feel a little bit shy, but okay.

THERAPIST: How does shy feel in your body?

HOPE: Shy can bring tears to my eyes, but not now. It's a little hard to look at you.

THERAPIST: Does your mouth get more or less dry when we talk about this?

HOPE: Less dry.

This indicated a reduction in sympathetic arousal, which meant we could go on.

THERAPIST: Have you thought about who you would like to put by the stream?

HOPE: Yes, my grandmother.

THERAPIST: How did you decide to choose her?

HOPE: We were very close. I could always go to her when I was upset. She was also the one who taught me to cook. We spent a lot of time in her kitchen. And she liked it down at the stream. We'd sometimes go there with a picnic, just us two.

Many people choose a grandparent for their safe person. What is important is that the client felt/feels safe with the person and that there are not too many complications. For example, if Hope had chosen her recently deceased husband, I might have discouraged her from using him here, at least to begin with, as her emotions were still too volatile when she thought about him. By the end of her therapy, though, when she is feeling more adjusted to his death and further along her grieving process, it may be possible to bring in her memories of him to enhance her feelings of safety.

THERAPIST: How do you feel talking about her?

HOPE: Very calm. A little sad; I still miss her.

Sad was fine, parasympathetic.

THERAPIST: Where will you imagine she waits for you?

HOPE: She'll be standing by the shore here (*points to her drawing*).

THERAPIST: What do you want her to do as you run toward her?

HOPE: I want her to open her arms and then embrace me.

THERAPIST: What would you like for her to say?

HOPE: Hmm . . . what she often said as she hugged me: "Oh, Hope, my little hope."

THERAPIST: How do you feel when you remember that?

HOPE: Warm in my chest, loved, a little sad. I meant a lot to her, and she to me.

THERAPIST: You might be running there with a certain amount of distress and fear. Imagine her saying that and embracing you. Is that the kind of reception you'll need in that condition or is there something else?

HOPE: Yes, that's good.

THERAPIST: Something just happened.

HOPE: My eyes are teary. I long for that kind of reassurance.

THERAPIST: What are you feeling?

HOPE: Sad.

THERAPIST: Longing to feel comfort?

HOPE: Yes (*crying*).

THERAPIST: Imagine, again, your grandmother saying, "Oh, Hope, my little hope," and see how you feel.

HOPE: It helps. I feel calm.

THERAPIST: You know, you can hear her say that anytime you want?

HOPE: I forget. I forget it's possible.

THERAPIST: All right, shall we try it? Maybe that will help you to remember.

HOPE: Yes.

THERAPIST: So for that I need to borrow your paper, if that is okay, and we need a way to get started. Do you want me to say, "Ready, set, go?"

HOPE: Yes, that's good. I might never start otherwise.

THERAPIST: Keep your feet flat on the floor. That will give you a better position for the imagined sensation of running. Okay? Ready, set, go. (*firmly and quickly*) Imagine you run right out the door and out of the building. You feel your legs are strong and they carry you quickly down the street. You turn left and keep running. Feel how strong your legs are as you run along. Up to the crosswalk and over Maple Street. Keep running; your legs are strong. Feel your feet hit the ground. You run under the bridge through to the other side, through the traffic light and right up to the magic carpet. You jump onto the magic carpet, run along it, and jump off just at the oak tree. You run down the path to the fence, still feeling your legs strong and feeling how fast they can carry you. You climb over the fence and continue running down the path to where your grandmother is waiting for you. As you approach her she opens her arms to embrace you and you hear her say, "Oh, Hope, my little hope."

This took about 1½ minutes. The idea is to help the client to imagine the sensation of running and to encourage her to keep going. Once the client is at the safe place, giving her cues to feel and hear the comforting person also helps.

HOPE: (*She cries.*)

THERAPIST: (*more slowly and gently*) Hear your grandmother. Feel her arms . . . . You can hear her say it again, she can repeat it. She might say something else . . . . Tell me what's happening.

HOPE: It felt good for a while. When she reached out for me I felt great, but then it stopped—that's why I'm sad.

THERAPIST: Do you know why it stopped?

HOPE: It just stopped because it sounded like it was over. Maybe it was relief.

THERAPIST: What are you feeling right now in your body?

HOPE: Some hotness in my back, my feet are quite cold. I got mixed up when I lost it.

We needed to take a look at what happened. It is crucial to emphasize that it is her fantasy and she can control it.

THERAPIST: What do you think happened?

HOPE: Something happened in my feet that made me go away. Yeah, that makes sense.

It did not make sense to me, but because it did to her, I went along.

THERAPIST: What happens when you think about that, does it change anything in your legs or in your feet?

HOPE: Less tension in my shins.

THERAPIST: Do you know what you need?

HOPE: Something more from my grandmother, but I don't know what.

THERAPIST: Well, she could say something more, or she could repeat her greeting and not just say it once.

HOPE: I think "You're safe now." Something like that, more reassurance. Add that to her greeting.

THERAPIST: "Oh, Hope, my little hope. You are safe now." (*Voice rising to indicate a question in the statement.*)

HOPE: Yes (*sighs*).

THERAPIST: Did you feel the sigh?

HOPE: Yes. That feels right. I can breathe easier.

THERAPIST: And how do you feel when you imagine her saying that?

HOPE: Less scared.

THERAPIST: How about you just try the last part from the oak tree with the enhanced greeting and see how that feels. Would that be all right?

HOPE: Okay.

It seemed that the arrival at the safe place into the arms of the comforting person was most important, more so than the running. That is often the case in the beginning. When care is taken to create just the right place, person, and reception, the rest of the work goes more easily.

THERAPIST: Are you ready?

HOPE: Yes.

THERAPIST: So, from the oak tree you run along the path. You climb over the fence and run to the stream where your grandmother is standing and waiting for you. She puts out her arms and embraces you. She says, "Oh, Hope, my little hope. You are safe now."

HOPE: (*sighs again*) Yes, that feels better.

THERAPIST: How?

HOPE: I feel more solid.

THERAPIST: How does that feel in your body?

THERAPIST: Much less anxious, my feet are warmer. But, I want to change the route, just a little bit. Is that okay?

THERAPIST: Yes, of course, it's your route!

It was nice to have her take control.

HOPE: Instead of going all the way down that path, there was a trail of stones across the part of the stream closer to my house. I often crossed the stones.

THERAPIST: Oh, okay.

HOPE: I forgot that.

THERAPIST: It sounds important. Do you want to try that part before we stop?

HOPE: Yes, please.

THERAPIST: From the oak tree?

HOPE: Yes.

THERAPIST: All right, run from the oak tree down the path and climb over the fence and then down to the stones. Run over them and then continue down the path to where your grandmother waits by the stream. You run up to her and she embraces you. She says, "Oh, Hope, my little hope. You are safe now."

HOPE: (*smiling*) I can picture it. Yeah!

THERAPIST: Tell me how you feel?

HOPE: (*very happy*) I feel good!

THERAPIST: You made it.

HOPE: I made it, yeah . . . . It felt like I hadn't made it before. I feel much more relaxed, really relieved.

Sometimes a small detail can be very important.

THERAPIST: What do you think happened?

HOPE: I think somewhere I was afraid I couldn't do it.

THERAPIST: So now you know you can?

HOPE: (*sighs*) Yes. Thank you.

THERAPIST: Are you pleased? (*She looks pleased.*)

HOPE: Very pleased.

This session was not meant to cure Hope of her grief or fear. What it did, though, was reacquaint her with feelings of safety and unconditional love that she had known in her childhood and youth. Because of the shock of her husband's death and her isolation in the wake of that, she had forgotten what "loved" and "safe" felt like. Without that internalized safe place, she was constantly scared as she could no longer tell the difference between safety and danger. Being able to imagine a place of safety and the comfort of her grandmother helped her to make this distinction. More work was needed in that area, but this session was a good start.

CHAPTER FOURTEEN

Traumatic Parenting

EMDR, TRANSACTIONAL ANALYSIS

In this course of therapy, I utilized techniques from EMDR to help the client resolve a childhood beating. I then applied theory from TA to help the client to nurture himself and to project nurturing his future children.

Josh, a man in his early thirties, came to therapy anxiously facing what he hoped would be an exciting change in his life: His wife was pregnant with their first child; they hoped to eventually have three. Instead of being happy, he was terribly afraid. He worried about his temper, about how he might treat his children when he became angry. He had mostly managed his explosive temper until now with forceful physical activity. Working out daily and spending weekends playing racquetball, soccer, and football helped him to "lengthen my wick," as he put it. So far his anger had not been a major problem in his marriage; his wife was good at standing up for herself. But he could see signs that it could become a problem with his children.

The incident that brought him to therapy involved one of their pets. A month before, his 9-month-old puppy had chewed up one of his favorite shoes. Josh had become very angry and hit the dog harshly several times. For days, the puppy avoided him. Josh felt ashamed and remorseful. He truly liked the dog and hadn't meant to hurt him, only to set a limit. But what bothered Josh most of all was that he had lost control.

At our first meeting Josh confided that he was afraid he could do something like that to a child. Intellectually, he knew he valued his dog over the shoe, and he knew he would value his children over material things. But he was afraid that when they broke or destroyed something of his (as is, he admitted, inevitable with children) he would lose his temper and harm them.

During the intake interview, a particular childhood incident stood out to both of us: At 10 years old, Josh was punished violently by his father. Though this was the sole occurrence of parental violence, the episode still haunted him. Josh had never forgotten what had happened, nor his feeling of being unjustly treated. He was aware that there were many parental issues to be resolved (his parents had divorced when he was 8), but he felt that this particular incident was central to his temper problems. By our fourth meeting Josh felt ready to address it.

We discussed the pros and cons of different methods. Josh had heard about EMDR and wanted to try it. I agreed that it was a good choice for him. Though he had endured a few other traumatic events in his life, he was able to keep them separate—typical of a Type IIA client—which made EMDR a safe choice of method.

THE EMDR PROTOCOL

Processing with EMDR involves setting up a protocol with the following questions (Shapiro, 1995, pp. 130–137):

1. Choose an aspect of the trauma to work on first. What image represents the issue or central aspect of the issue?

2. When you concentrate on that image, how do you feel about yourself *now*? This is referred to as the *negative cognition*.

3. How would you rather think about yourself when you remember [chosen aspect] in the future? This is referred to as the *positive cognition*.

4. How true does the positive cognition feel? Rank it on a scale of 1 (not at all true) to 7 (absolutely true). This is referred to as the *validity of cognition* (VOC).

5. When you concentrate on the image, what emotion do you feel?

6. How distressed do you feel right now? Rank it on scale of 1 (perfectly calm) to 10 (worst upset possible). This is referred to as the *SUDS* (subjective units of distress scale; Wolpe, 1969).

7. Where in your body do you feel that distress?

As a side note, it can be seen that the elements of the EMDR protocol closely approximate the elements of Levine's SIBAM. The only inconsistency is the missing "B" for behavior. Two questions that could be added to the EMDR protocol are: What movement impulses activate when you remember that scene? Where in your body do you feel those impulses?

Once these questions are answered, the protocol progresses to desensitization and reprocessing using sets of bilateral stimulation—traditionally right-left eye movements, but sometimes alternating sounds (via earphones) or alternating tapping of hands or knees. The process begins with the image, negative cognition, emotion, and body sensations identified by the previous questions. As desensitization and reprocessing continues, the thoughts, images, sensations, and emotions change, eventually resolving the original issue or trauma. The course of the therapy session proceeds with client reports and additional bilateral stimulation until both client and therapist judge that the trauma has been fully processed: usually when the client is no longer distressed when remembering the incident (SUDS = 1 or 2) and when the validity of the positive cognition increases (VOC = 6 or 7). Sometimes the disturbing images disappear or become dull.

THE THERAPY

Josh Outlines the Trauma

Josh's parents divorced when he was 8. They shared custody of Josh, and he alternated his stays with them on a weekly basis. At his father's home, Josh was responsible for keeping his own room and the living room orderly (a cleaning lady came once a week for major cleaning; his father did everything else). Josh's father came home around 6 P.M. and brought or made dinner (he was a good cook). One afternoon when Josh was 10 years old, he was straightening up the living room and broke one of his father's favorite pipes. He tried to repair it with glue, but it was beyond hope so he threw it away and forgot about it. When his father discovered the pipe in the trash he flew into a rage, grabbed Josh from the couch where he had been sitting, and spanked him severely. Josh cried from pain and fear. He tried to explain what had happened and apologize, but his father wouldn't listen. Josh was sent to his room without supper that night. The next morning his father acted as though nothing had happened. Josh tried again to apologize, but his father changed the subject. Josh went to school as usual and tried to put the event behind him, as he saw no way to make amends with his father.

The worst scene for Josh was when he tried to tell his father what had happened while being spanked. Contrary to the standard EMDR philosophy, I prefer to work first with events following the traumatic event rather than with the most disturbing memory. I believed that Josh would get more mileage out of work with the most disturbing memory once he had built some resources that had not been available to him at the time.

First Trauma Session

We began the first trauma session by talking about how Josh had felt at school the next morning. He was ashamed, hurt, and isolated. He had gotten into a fight with one of his good friends over "nothing." We decided to target this aspect of the trauma and began to construct the standard EMDR protocol.

1. Image: Scene at school; picking fight with friend.

2. Negative cognition: I'm all alone; there is no one on my side.

3. Positive cognition: I'm not alone; I have friends.

4. VOC: 3.

5. Emotion: Sadness.

6. SUDS: 6.

7. Body sensation: He feels the sadness as tightness in his throat and chest.

For the bilateral stimulation he chose to use a device that delivers alternating tones through earphones. I asked him to focus on the seven points just listed and turned on the tones for 30 seconds. I then instructed him to take a deep breath and tell me what had emerged in his thoughts, emotions, and/or body sensations.

We repeated this process several times over the next 30 minutes: At each step new insights or emotional or body changes emerged. We followed these by additional alternating tones. Josh quickly grasped that he had picked a fight with his friend because he had felt so angry and hurt about his father. He remembered that he had actually wanted to tell his friend what had happened but feared his friend would laugh at him for getting spanked; he was afraid of feeling further humiliated. Toward the end of the processing he remembered that later in the friendship his friend had once confided being hit by older siblings. This led Josh to realize that the friend might have been able to be supportive, had he dared tell him. I encouraged him to imagine telling his friend what had happened. He cried while doing so. Afterward, his tight throat and chest were much relieved.

Second Trauma Session

After the first trauma session Josh talked with his wife about what had happened with his father and the isolation he'd felt the next day. His wife remarked that he still did the same thing, keeping his feelings bottled up and rarely sharing them with friends. We spent much of this session strategizing about how he could change this pattern.

Third Trauma Session

Josh was ready to tackle another upsetting scene from the morning following the spanking. His father's refusal to talk about the incident had distressed him immensely. It had caused Josh to doubt his own reality: Had it really been so bad? He worried that he was making a mountain out of a molehill.

We set up the EMDR protocol:

1. Image: Trying to apologize to his father at breakfast; his father looking away and changing the subject.

2. Negative cognition: There must be something wrong with me; I can never get it right.

3. Positive cognition: There's nothing wrong with me.

4. VOC: 2.

5. Emotion: Shame.

6. SUDS: 8.

7. Body sensation: Warm cheeks, shallow respiration.

This image was more difficult to process. Josh's shame was very strong and kept returning to focus even as other bits were resolved. It is common in EMDR for the client to continue processing a memory without any input from the therapist. But because Josh was getting stuck, I thought intervention was warranted. In EMDR a "cognitive interweave" is used in such a situation (Shapiro, 1995, pp. 244–271). Basically, it is the kind of intervention that most psychodynamic psychotherapists would recognize as an invitation for the client to look at the situation from a different angle. In this case I asked Josh what feelings he thought were causing his father's evasive behavior: "Why do you think your father wouldn't look at you?" That really threw him. He'd assumed his father was still angry. But upon closer examination he remembered that when his father was angry he lectured and yelled—both things he did while looking directly at Josh. For the first time Josh considered the possibility that his father's evasion might have meant something else.

I encouraged Josh to think about that while I turned on the alternating tones. Josh emerged from that moment of focus with a growing astonishment. "You know, if I didn't know my father better, I might think he was embarrassed." "Think about that," I told him, and I turned on more tones.

After a few more minutes Josh said, "He *was* embarrassed! He was embarrassed he hit me, that he lost control. He had never spanked me before, and he never did it after that. I thought it was because I was careful not to do anything to provoke him. But of course I did, I was just a kid. He was embarrassed that he hit me, and he couldn't face me and he couldn't apologize!"

That insight changed the situation for Josh completely. He had never realized his father had regretted the beating. We discussed the possibility of Josh speaking with his dad *now* about what had happened. Josh thought it was a good idea, but knew he would be nervous about it.

Fourth Trauma Session

Between sessions Josh called his father and arrived at our next session feeling satisfied. Their conversation had been productive, albeit challenging. We agreed it was probably better for both of them to have opened this up over the phone rather than in person, as they were each feeling so much shame. They were both surprised that the other remembered the incident so well.

Josh's father acknowledged that he had, indeed, been embarrassed about losing his temper over a broken pipe. He also felt he had been in a bind: The morning after he had been afraid that if he apologized, Josh might become indifferent to other people's property. He had regretted the beating, but wanted the boy to be more careful. This was as far as they got. It was the most intimate conversation they had had in years. Josh was pleased that he had dared to broach the subject, and that his father had been able to respond. Even though he had not exactly apologized, he had come close enough to satisfy Josh.

We spent the rest of this session talking, helping Josh to integrate this change in his relationship with his father.

Fifth Trauma Session

After digesting the conversation with his father, Josh felt ready to tackle the worst part of the trauma: getting spanked while he tried to explain what had happened. We set up the EMDR protocol:

1. Image: Being turned over his father's knee.

2. Negative cognition: I screwed up; I'm bad.

3. Positive cognition: I'm human; I made a mistake.

4. VOC: 5.

5. Emotion: Anger, humiliation.

6. SUDS: 4.

7. Body sensation: Tense shoulders, burning buttocks.

The low SUDS and high VOC were indicative of the impact of the previous sessions. Had we approached this scene first thing, it is likely that the VOC would have been much lower and the SUDS much higher.

Processing the scene (in the same manner as previous sessions) brought Josh to a place of being stuck. He couldn't get past feeling that he had done something very wrong. At this point I believed that interfacing another model with the EMDR could be useful. From TA I introduced the idea of *reparenting*—learning to be a good parent toward himself. I suspected this could be useful in resolving the memory and also in making an imprint for his future parenting of his own children.

I suggested that Josh imagine taking his current adult self into the scene as the parent. How would he handle the situation of finding the broken pipe?

After a few moments, Josh knew what he would do. He would have asked the boy what had happened. Most importantly, he would have *listened* to the answer. If he judged that the incident was truly an accident, he would have put his arm around the boy and said, "It's okay. Accidents happen, but next time tell me instead of just throwing it away." If he found that the boy had done it to express anger, he would have talked with him about it and offered alternative strategies for dealing with anger. He also would have asked the boy to pay for it out of his allowance or money earned for chores, especially if he had been breaking things repeatedly. This would teach him the consequences of not being careful.

Josh concluded with a smile on his face: "Yes, that's how I want to be with my children. I don't want things to matter more than my relationship with my kids. Of course, I want them to respect property, but accidents do happen. I don't want to be as hard on them as my father was on me. I want it to be okay for my kids to screw up once in a while." He focused on those words and his smile while I turned on the tones for a few seconds.

Over the next few weeks, Josh had the opportunity to observe whether this part of his therapy had affected his ability to control his temper. The dog, although over a year old now, was still mischievous and had angered or frustrated Josh several times. One night it spread trash all over the kitchen while Josh and his wife were out to dinner. Josh yelled at the dog but didn't come close to hitting it. Josh knew that children could be even more trying at times, but this incident helped him to feel confident about holding his temper in check.

CHAPTER FIFTEEN

Changing Perspective

LEVINE'S SIBAM MODEL

This chapter illustrates how the SIBAM model, first developed for understanding dissociation, can be applied to process a traumatic incident and increase association of forgotten or dissociated aspects. As noted earlier, the goal of trauma therapy is to integrate the aspects of the trauma—the sensation, image, behavior, affect, and meaning—bringing them into consciousness and creating a cohesive narrative. These elements will be labeled in the transcript.

Using the SIBAM model involves a three part process:

1. Through listening, observation, and inquiry, identify which elements of the experience the client is consciously aware of.

2. Identify the elements that are either missing (not mentioned) or not in the client's consciousness (i.e., movement or emotional ex-

pression may be observed by the therapist but outside the realm of the client's consciousness).

3. Ask questions and/or give feedback in order to bring the missing elements into conscious awareness, and then help to make sense of them within the context of the trauma.

The final goal that I find most helpful is for the client to realize a culminating meaning that makes sense of how the trauma has affected her. On this point, my opinion differs from Levine's. He believes that the most important factor is completing physical movements (behaviors) that were frustrated during the trauma (Levine, 1992, 1997). Although I agree that working with impeded movement is a valuable part of the process, I have observed that it is the epiphany of meaning—the "ah ha"—that severs the trauma's hold.

Using the SIBAM model enables very fine control, as if you have one foot on the brake and one on the accelerator at all times. Arousal can easily be increased or reduced as needed. That makes using this model well suited to clients whose stability is unpredictable, or who are too fragile to consider a model less easy to control. It is also a good model to use with someone who is skeptical of therapy or mechanical equipment. With the SIBAM model, there is no specific protocol to follow or specific procedures to insert.

Larry was 42 when he first experienced a violent incident. His used-book store was burglarized. It was a seemingly minor incident: The burglar had only broken the backdoor lock and stolen some petty cash. Nonetheless, much to his dismay, a year later Larry was still very bothered by it. He obsessively rechecked the locks before leaving every night, and each morning he had an upset stomach until he arrived at the store and saw that it was intact. This was the first time Larry had experienced such an intrusion and he feared what else could befall him. His life was becoming more restricted, as he also began to worry about potential break-ins at home. Fearing what could happen while he was gone, he no longer liked going out in the evenings.

Larry had never been in therapy before and was skeptical of anything that smacked of technique. For that reason, I believed he was well suited to the SIBAM model. I also thought it was a good pick because I was uncertain of his level of stability: The degree to which Larry had been debilitated seemed disproportionate to his resource-filled history and the severity of the trauma. I was concerned that there might be some difficulty lurking unseen and wanted to use a method that could control for such possible surprises. In the end, that did not prove to be the case, though nonetheless, the SIBAM model proved to be a good choice.

My first meeting with Larry focused on his history, and the second was dedicated to equipping him with skills to put on the brakes. The following transcript begins with our third meeting.

LARRY: I'd like to get started, to see if I can finally lay this to rest.

THERAPIST: Okay. But first I want to make sure that we have something pleasant, an anchor, to talk about to help modulate your stress level while we work on this.

LARRY: I'm already stressed. I feel pretty nervous. This has been going on a long time.

Many clients come into therapy with the accelerator already down, hyperarousal symptoms strong. The first task is to calm them so that the difficult work of addressing traumatic memories can start from a calmer place.

THERAPIST: Can you tell me what that nervousness feels like in your body? For example, is your heart beating fast?

LARRY: It's hammering away. And my hands are sweaty—that kind of thing?

THERAPIST: Yes, exactly. Anything else?

LARRY: That's what stands out.

THERAPIST: Well, what do you like to talk about? Something that makes you feel calm or even happy.

An anchor is a good braking tool with any trauma therapy, but with the SIBAM model, it is a necessity to keep arousal from getting out of hand. It is one mechanism that makes this model easy to control. It is a good idea to choose an anchor that has all SIBAM elements available to the client's consciousness, as illustrated in the following dialogue.

LARRY: I like to talk about cars. My wife is sick of hearing me go on about them, but I love cars.

THERAPIST: Just when you name that topic, something changes in you. Can you feel it?

LARRY: I know I'm smiling (*behavior*). Oh, and I can feel my hands are suddenly dryer (*sensation*).

THERAPIST: How about your heartrate?

LARRY: Now that you mention it, it's slowed down (*behavior*).

THERAPIST: How do you feel when we switch the topic to cars?

LARRY: Relaxed (*behavior*) and happy (*affect*).

THERAPIST: Do you know what it is about you and cars?

LARRY: I guess I never really thought about it a lot. It's a guy thing, I guess. I've liked them since I was really little (*meaning*). I can remember building model cars and how they lined my room (*image*).

THERAPIST: How are you feeling?

LARRY: Much calmer. And sort of surprised.

THERAPIST: Why is that?

LARRY: I just expected we would forge ahead with the burglary and I would just get more and more upset. It surprises me you want me to calm down first.

THERAPIST: Do you understand the reason?

LARRY: Not really, but I'll go along with it. Just so as I can get over this burglary.

THERAPIST: Well, of course I can't promise you that. But by helping you to find things that are calming, and encouraging you to pay attention to your body sensations, you will be the best judge of what is helping you toward that goal and what is not.

LARRY: Aren't you going to tell me what is best?

THERAPIST: I'm certainly going to guide you based on my experience and knowledge. But ultimately, it will be you who determines what helps. A doctor can prescribe penicillin, but only the patient can feel if the sore throat is really gone.

LARRY: Yeah, okay. That makes sense. Can we go on now?

THERAPIST: Yes, but I have a couple more questions about cars, first. Is there anything in particular you would like for me to ask you about when we switch to talking about cars?

LARRY: Nah, just ask away. You can ask about my car or yours, or ask me about the car show I went to last week. That was fantastic!

THERAPIST: Who did you go with—your wife?

I took advantage of the opportunity to assess his relationship.

LARRY: No way! She hates my obsession. But she never stops me from going to see them or from reading about them. And I have plenty of buddies to talk with.

THERAPIST: So you don't mind that she doesn't like cars?

LARRY: No. We have plenty of other things to talk about, and I don't like to hear about some of her girlish interests, so we're even.

As well as establishing a useful anchor, within a matter of a few minutes I had confirmed what he told me during the intake interview: that he had a good and mutually supportive relationship with his wife and a network of friends. This was useful information, as interpersonal support is a great help in the resolution of trauma.

THERAPIST: Okay, why don't you tell me what's been bothering you about the burglary.

LARRY: I keep remembering the state of the store. The bathroom window and backdoor were both left wide open.

THERAPIST: Is this something you actually saw?

LARRY: Yes, when I arrived on the scene. The security company had called me when the alarm went off. The lock was broken, and the rear window and door stood wide open.

THERAPIST: What are you feeling right now?

LARRY: It's sort of hard to breathe (*behavior*).

THERAPIST: You look like you've stopped moving; is that right?

LARRY: Yeah, I sort of feel like I can't move (*behavior*).

THERAPIST: Tell me how you experience that and where.

LARRY: I can't move my face; it's frozen (*behavior*).

THERAPIST: What does that feel like?

LARRY: Sort of numb (*sensation*).

Probably from hyperarousal.

THERAPIST: I think it'll be a good idea to use your anchor. So, what kind of car do you have?

LARRY: A red 1976 Mustang. It's a classic.

THERAPIST: Wow, a great car! When did you get it?

LARRY: I'm the original owner. Actually, my parents gave it to me my sophomore year in college. It's my transportation and my hobby. I keep it running perfectly.

THERAPIST: So, how are you feeling right now?

LARRY: I love talking about my car.

I asked about affect and he responded with an exclamation. He did that a lot—responding with something else when asked about sensation and emotion. I needed to be more specific with my questions.

THERAPIST: How does that feel in your body?

LARRY: I can breathe (*behavior*) and my hands are warm (*sensation*).

He answered that question easily. It may be that the crossed communication came more from my questions than from any evasiveness on his part. I needed to pay attention to my wording.

THERAPIST: And the frozenness in your face?

LARRY: Gone. I can move it (*demonstrates by making some faces*).

THERAPIST: Let's go back to the burglary. What continues to disturb you about it?

LARRY: I keep seeing the open door and window (*image*).

THERAPIST: And how does that make you feel?

LARRY: Vulnerable (*meaning*)! Like anyone can get in.

In this usage, "vulnerable" was a meaning, how he named a combination of sensations and emotions. At this point I wanted to know the emotion.

THERAPIST: What emotion goes with the vulnerable?

LARRY: Scared. I feel scared (*affect*).

THERAPIST: What happens when you talk about it now?

LARRY: I feel sort of shocked (*meaning*).

Also a combination state, like "vulnerable."

THERAPIST: Can you be more specific? Can you tell me what that means? Because somebody else might mean something different by "shocked."

LARRY: I'm nauseous (*sensation*).

THERAPIST: What else happens in your body as you see this image?

LARRY: Tightening up in my shoulders, and my hands clench (*behavior*). But actually I don't feel my body much (*sensation*).

THERAPIST: What I hear is that you describe mostly movement but few sensations. Is that what you mean by not having contact with your body?

LARRY: Yes, it feels a bit frozen, like my face did before.

At this point I assessed that Larry spoke a lot about images, his body's move-ments (or absence of movement, like frozenness), and interpretations (mean-ings). I was not hearing or seeing much in the way of awareness of body sensations, and little of emotions. This helped point me in the direction of questions that would bring some of those elements into his consciousness. If that was done correctly, the experience would coalesce, making it possible for him to make sense of what had been disturbing him.

THERAPIST: When you feel the frozenness and see that image, what are you aware of emotionally?

LARRY: Afraid. Angry. Both (*affect*).

THERAPIST: Also when you tense up?

LARRY: Yes.

THERAPIST: What are the sensations in your body that indicate you are both afraid and angry?

LARRY: What do you mean by sensations that indicate I'm angry and afraid?

Emotions are actually composed of body sensations, although many people never notice this.

THERAPIST: Sensations and emotions go hand in hand. Like butterflies in your stomach when you are nervous or a hot face when you are embarrassed. What sensations are you aware of now?

LARRY: My hands hurt, and well, like you said, there are butterflies in my stomach (*sensation*).

THERAPIST: How angry are you?

LARRY: (*strongly*) I could knock his damn head off, is that what you mean (*affect and meaning*)?

THERAPIST: And what happens in your hands when you raise your voice and tell me that?

LARRY: They clench (*behavior*).

THERAPIST: Does that feel good, bad, or neutral?

LARRY: Actually, it feels sort of good.

THERAPIST: What might your hands want to do?

LARRY: I really would like to hit him, I can feel that in my hands (*behavior*).

THERAPIST: Can you imagine that—what it would feel like in your arms and your hands?

LARRY: It actually feels good, I'm less numb (*sensation*).

THERAPIST: What else do you notice?

LARRY: Well, I'm not as scared (*affect*).

THERAPIST: Let's return to that image of the open door and window. What happens?

LARRY: I get a little numb again (*sensation*). And the picture is frozen, standing still (*image*).

THERAPIST: Let's move back to your anchor. What's your favorite kind of car?

We talked about cars for a couple of minutes.

THERAPIST: What is happening in your body?

LARRY: I feel more relaxed, I can breathe.

THERAPIST: Can you make an image of your favorite car?

LARRY: Yes.

THERAPIST: Okay, then go back to the image that has been frightening you. What happens?

LARRY: I'm holding my breath again (*behavior*).

THERAPIST: Good. Now go back to the image of your favorite car. What happens?

LARRY: (*exhales deeply*)

THERAPIST: Could you feel that?

LARRY: Yes, I can breath (*behavior*)! It's like getting uncorked (*meaning*).

THERAPIST: Do you know why I'm having you do this?

I wanted Larry to know my motivations. Hopefully my rationale would help his thinking. If he didn't know the answer, I would tell him—I didn't want to engage in a guessing game.

LARRY: I guess so—I can choose.

THERAPIST: Yes, we are putting you back in the driver's seat, so to speak. Do you know what it is that upsets you about that image?

LARRY: When I see that I feel like anyone can get in (*meaning*).

THERAPIST: What does that feel like?

LARRY: I feel vulnerable (*meaning*).

THERAPIST: What else?

LARRY: Scared (*affect*). My hands are sweaty (*sensation*).

THERAPIST: Of course, the burglary would remind you of your vulnerability. You have the image of the open door and the thought that anything can get in, so you feel vulnerable. How does that feel in your body?

LARRY: Very soft in my chest (*sensation*).

THERAPIST: And the image now?

LARRY: Of the burglar. He's there even though I never saw him.

THERAPIST: What do you imagine?

LARRY: That he's arrogant, doesn't give a damn. He thinks he's invulnerable (*meaning*). That's what scares me so much.

THERAPIST: When you talk about that, it seems like there's something that happens in your body.

LARRY: I'm shivering (*behavior*); I feel cold (*sensation*).

THERAPIST: So, stay with those feelings a little while.

The shivering would discharge some of his anxiety and make it easier to think.

THERAPIST: How are you feeling now?

LARRY: I'm warming up a little. Not so shaky.

THERAPIST: Do you think that he believes he's invulnerable when he's breaking into your store?

LARRY: Of course, otherwise he wouldn't try it (*meaning*).

THERAPIST: Then why would he leave the door and window open?

With this question, I challenged Larry's logic. It is difficult to associate such an intervention with a particular model. Probably the root of the idea comes from CBT. In EMDR it would be called a "cognitive interweave." But such interventions often have roots in how we as therapists think in general. For me at that moment, the question just seemed like common sense.

LARRY: Well, maybe somewhere along the line he really didn't want to get caught (*meaning*).

This was an important change in his thinking, but it was not integrated yet.

THERAPIST: What do you feel in your body when you say that?

LARRY: (*pointing to upper chest*) A sensation here (*sensation*).

THERAPIST: Can you describe it?

LARRY: Well, painful, and lots of tightness in my back (*sensation*).

THERAPIST: And when you think about him being arrogant and not giving a damn, and feel the pain in your chest and tightness in your back, what emotions do you feel?

I tied the elements together.

LARRY: Scared (*affect*), and like I don't really exist (*meaning*).

THERAPIST: Don't exist to whom?

LARRY: To the burglar. As far as he's concerned, I didn't exist. Only the money in my store existed for him (*meaning*).

THERAPIST: What are your hands doing?

LARRY: They're clenched (*behavior*). What a bastard (*affect and meaning*)!

THERAPIST: How do you feel when you say those words?

LARRY: Angry, it's an outrage (*affect and meaning*)!

THERAPIST: What happens to the frozenness when you feel that anger and say, "It's an outrage." (*Voice rising to indicate a question.*)

LARRY: I feel less frozen (*behavior*).

THERAPIST: How?

LARRY: My back is looser (*behavior*) and my chest doesn't hurt so much (*sensation*).

THERAPIST: Do you have any fantasies now about him?

I checked to see if there was any integration yet.

LARRY: Well, I wonder if he was scared because he took a lot of precautions (*meaning*). He blockaded the front door, turned off the alarm, and kept the back door and window open (*image*).

Now he was thinking more clearly, connecting his information to a different view.

THERAPIST: Why do you think he did all that?

LARRY: Maybe so he'd be able to escape if he was caught (*meaning*)?

This was the beginnings of an epiphany, a new way to think about the event.

THERAPIST: Is that a question?

LARRY: No, I think it's right, I'd just not thought of that before.

THERAPIST: It sounds like it means something to you that he took all these precautions, that he might have been afraid. Something just shifted in your eyes, what's happening?

LARRY: Something weird. The image of the door changed. It looks the same (*image*), but it occurs to me that it's open to let him *out*, not to let everyone else in (*meaning*).

This was integration: The image changed, and with it the meaning.

THERAPIST: That's quite a change. How does it feel in your face?

LARRY: *Much* better.

THERAPIST: What's much better? Can you describe your sensations now? Before it was frozen.

LARRY: It feels softer (*sensation*), I can move the muscles in my face. (*behavior*). (*He moves his face around.*)

With the changed image and meaning, there were associated changes in his body.

THERAPIST: I see you laughing . . . . Tell me about it.

LARRY: It's really good to realize that. Don't know why I didn't think of it before! Would have saved me *lots* of money (*meaning*).

THERAPIST: What are you feeling?

LARRY: Relieved, and like I'd like to give him a big kick in the ass (*meaning*).

THERAPIST: How does that feel in your body?

LARRY: My right leg feels really strong (*sensation*). It's my kicking leg.

THERAPIST: Try some kicking motions with it; stand up if you like.

Larry made several kicks (behavior).

THERAPIST: How does that feel?

LARRY: Good. I feel more in charge, like I have myself back (*meaning*).

THERAPIST: Is this a good place to stop?

LARRY: Yes, I think so.

Larry came for another session to check that the changes from this one had held. He was astonished to find that he no longer feared going to work and that his worries about his home also had faded. He did take adequate security precautions—locks and alarms on both buildings—but his fears dissipated.

It is important to emphasize here that the speed of the therapy in this case was largely due to Larry's basically stable psychological state prior to the incident. He had many resources to fall back on. The burglary knocked him off balance, but it didn't knock him over. Had the same incident occurred with someone with fewer resources and/or who was more fragile to start with, the healing might have taken longer and been more complicated.

CHAPTER SIXTEEN

Out of Isolation

SOMATIC TRAUMA THERAPY, COGNITIVE BEHAVIORAL THERAPY, ATTACHMENT THEORY

Victims of trauma often feel very isolated, especially when the traumatic event was experienced alone. The feeling of separateness can be compounded if, for whatever reason, the victim does not feel he can tell anyone what happened.

Kjell was married and in his mid-fifties. He had been my client for 2 months. The session transcribed here was the first of four addressing the incident discussed below.* Major strategies include the use of somatic trauma therapy to integrate a major aspect of the trauma—in this case, isolation—with liberal use of brakes to prevent overwhelm, and behavioral methods (CBT) to help the client to reestablish attachment and reach out for contact.

*A version of this case was published previously (Rothschild, 2002a).

THERAPIST: Is how are we sitting—this distance and positioning—okay with you?

KJELL: It's fine.

THERAPIST: What's happening in your body?

I used body awareness as a guide to set up the therapeutic space. This was also a good way to train body awareness.

KJELL: A little excitement.

THERAPIST: What are the body sensations?

KJELL: My heart's beating faster and I'm shaking a little.

This sounded like anxiety to me.

THERAPIST: I suggest you experiment with the distance between us.

Kjell moved his chair back from me about one foot.

THERAPIST: What happens to your heartbeat and shaking when you move your chair back?

KJELL: Better now. Both are less.

THERAPIST: What does that tell you?

I was making sense of the change in sensations: mind/body integration.

KJELL: I was sitting too close to you. I'm more comfortable now.

THERAPIST: Okay. Tell me just the title of what you want to work on.

This is a strategy for pacing entry into work with the trauma. We went in one step at a time instead of jumping in with both feet.

KJELL: "A close call—too close!"

THERAPIST: What happens in your body when you say that?

KJELL: It becomes more tense.

Just naming the title was already activating. This is not uncommon and helps to alert both client and therapist to the importance of pacing.

THERAPIST: All over, or somewhere particular?

KJELL: Especially in my chest. It is hard to breathe.

THERAPIST: Is there anywhere that doesn't feel tense?

KJELL: I feel weak in my legs.

Trauma often gives a feeling of being "weak in the knees."

THERAPIST: Try pressing your feet into the floor so that your thighs tense up a little. Can you do that?

KJELL: Yes.

THERAPIST: What happens in your chest when you tense up in your thighs?

KJELL: My chest relaxes a little and I can breathe easier.

This is an example of using muscle tensing to mediate negative reactions. Bringing more strength to the legs made it possible for the overly tense chest to relax a little.

THERAPIST: Would you like to talk about what happened? Just the outline, first—the headings.

Again, I paced the telling of his story so that he could digest the pieces.

KJELL: Three years ago I was shot at by a sniper. I was driving in my car; he was on an overpass. I wasn't hurt—he just shot out my rear windshield. I called the police, but as no one had seen the sniper and he left no evidence, they couldn't do anything.

THERAPIST: What's happening in your body?

KJELL: Only a little tension.

It appeared to be okay to go on.

THERAPIST: Okay. What were the next steps?

KJELL: (*with shaking voice*) I stopped going out so much.

Kjell began to cry. A central issue had emerged.

THERAPIST: I see you are crying. Can you tell me what's happening—what you are feeling while you are crying?

I wanted Kjell to be able to think and feel at the same time—the goal of mind/body integration. Though I could observe him crying, I didn't know what emotion he was feeling.

KJELL: All mixed up.

THERAPIST: What feelings are mixed up?

KJELL: Being by myself. No one could help me. No one knew who it was. I didn't know if it could happen again.

Still no emotion was named.

THERAPIST: And so you are feeling?

KJELL: Like lost, completely lost.

He was describing his experience, not identifying an emotion. I decided to try to ask more specific questions.

THERAPIST: What are the sensations in your body?

KJELL: Like I am covered with a film.

THERAPIST: How do you experience that?

KJELL: I feel a bit numb. And you are a little blurry.

He was experiencing slight dissociation from his body. That probably was why he couldn't identify his emotions.

THERAPIST: Have you ever told anyone about what happened?

KJELL: My wife, but it scared her so much I never mentioned it again. And the police, but they couldn't do anything, so I gave up.

THERAPIST: It sounds as though you were quite isolated during that time.

KJELL: (*eyes watering*) I didn't know who to talk to. The police couldn't help me. I didn't want to scare my wife more. Because she got so scared, I was afraid to tell—and scare—anyone else. I didn't want to make a big deal out of nothing.

THERAPIST: What were your feelings then?

KJELL: I felt really scared.

He could identify his past emotion, which would help him to connect to his current emotion. He began to cry.

THERAPIST: Say that again.

KJELL: I was really scared.

Kjell cried more deeply. The sobs subsided after a while.

THERAPIST: What are you feeling as you cry?

KJELL: Scared.

THERAPIST: How are the feelings of being scared then and being scared now different?

KJELL: (*taking a deep breath*) Right now I can relax. Then I was just always wound up.

THERAPIST: Can you feel that difference in your body now?

KJELL: Yes. I can breathe!

THERAPIST: You never told anyone how scared you were?

KJELL: No, not really.

THERAPIST: Can you tell me?

KJELL: I was really scared.

He trembled a little.

THERAPIST: I see you are trembling. See if it can be okay to just let that happen.

Kjell continued to tremble for about 30 seconds.

THERAPIST: How do you feel?

KJELL: I feel more relaxed in my chest.

Something changed in Kjell's eyes.

THERAPIST: What is happening to your vision?

KJELL: I can see you more clearly.

THERAPIST: And the numbness?

KJELL: A little less.

Less dissociation from his body.

THERAPIST: What do you think that means?

KJELL: That I am a little less scared.

THERAPIST: Can you say more about that?

KJELL: After shaking and crying I can see you more clearly. I am relieved to have finally told someone.

THERAPIST: Do you think you could tell someone else?

It was important to help make a bridge out to Kjell's daily life, to decrease his sense of isolation there. Kjell's life had been threatened by the sniper, but the worst consequence was being isolated with his fear.

KJELL: That isn't easy for me.

THERAPIST: Do you know why?

KJELL: I'm sort of embarrassed to still be scared about something that happened 3 years ago.

THERAPIST: Is there anyone who might understand that?

KJELL: Probably my brother.

THERAPIST: How do you think he would respond to hearing your story?

KJELL: I think he would be empathetic. But he might also be irritated I never told him before.

THERAPIST: Do you think you could handle that?

KJELL: Yes.

THERAPIST: How might it feel to tell him?

KJELL: It might be a relief.

THERAPIST: Can you imagine telling him?

KJELL: Yes. I'm doing that.

THERAPIST: What happens when you imagine telling him? (*Kjell exhales deeply*.) Can you feel how much you are exhaling?

KJELL: It's reducing the pressure inside. I was so confused. I didn't want to scare anyone. I was so alone (*crying again*). Someone should have seen how scared I was.

THERAPIST: How do you feel when you say that?

KJELL: I feel angry. I was protecting everyone when I was needing support.

THERAPIST: What do you think about that now?

KJELL: I think it's about time I told someone.

THERAPIST: When?

KJELL: I'll call my brother tonight.

THERAPIST: How are you feeling in your body?

KJELL: Lighter. Relaxed. Relieved.

In subsequent sessions Kjell was also helped to talk with his wife and repair the rift that occurred at that time. Using somatic trauma therapy he was able to address his somatic response to having been shot at, releasing that anxiety from his body as well as from his mind.

CHAPTER SEVENTEEN

Running Away

BODYNAMIC RUNNING TECHNIQUE, NEURO-LINGUISTIC PROGRAMMING, TRANSACTIONAL ANALYSIS

Arlene came to therapy to resolve problems arising from a date rape she had experienced about 10 years before, when she was in her late teens. Like many woman in her situation, she was ashamed and never reported it to authorities. Both the trauma of the rape and the resulting guilt and shame required attention in therapy.

After the recent breakup of a particularly stormy relationship, Arlene began to realize that unresolved issues from the rape were preventing her from moving forward in her life. Now in her late twenties, she was ready to face what had happened. She enjoyed many resources and was close to her family. She was experiencing posttraumatic stress, not posttraumatic stress disorder. Arlene was still relatively functional, though there were areas of her life that were still suffering.

The fact of the rape had never been a secret, but Arlene had not been able to reveal the details to anyone. Although the rape did not intrude on her life on a daily basis, it did affect her sexual relationships, causing her to be easily startled and rather reserved. More generally, she had difficulty asserting limits and boundaries and often felt encroached on by others. She quickly grasped the relationship between the rape and her tendency to feel intrusion. And she knew that her problems with assertiveness existed before she was raped and possibly played a role in her having been vulnerable to that situation.

Arlene was a good candidate for imaginal use of the bodynamic running technique, as this event was appropriate for activating the flight reflex and she was otherwise fairly stable. I had given her the choice of several models, including EMDR and Levine's SIBAM model. She liked the idea of being able to imagine running away and decided she would like to try it. Though the bodynamic running technique was at the center of the therapy, interventions from NLP (neuro-linguistic programming) and TA (transactional analysis) were used to enhance its success.

Before approaching the memories of the rape, Arlene's therapy focused on building skills in containment and boundary-setting. The trauma work described here began a few months into the therapy.

FIRST TRAUMA SESSION

We dedicated the first trauma session to outlining the trauma. Outlining is a strategy for modulating the telling of the trauma narrative. It helps to prevent premature discussion of details that could lead to becoming overwhelmed or retraumatized. Once the outline is complete, the client and therapist have a structure they can use to address each point on an individual basis and decide which points to deal with first, second, third, etc. It is not necessary to take each point in order;

often it is a good idea *not* to. Addressing the easier points first can build the resources and courage to face those that are hardest. Eventually, though, it is necessary to put all points together into a complete narrative in order to integrate the trauma.

With my guidance, Arlene first gave the trauma a title: "The Rape." Next she outlined the progression:

1. "Pulled out of the car"

2. "Trapped in the living room"

3. and 4. (Arlene knew what these headings were, but she wasn't ready to name them aloud yet, so we left them blank.)

5. "Locking myself in the bathroom"

6. "Leaving the bathroom"

7. "Unlocking the front door"

8. "Driving home"

Each step of the way we paused to evaluate somatic symptoms. Her arousal level stayed low, so we kept going. (This isn't always the case, however. Some clients are so distressed that just naming the trauma, however briefly, causes hyperarousal. In those instances it is necessary to "put on the brakes" before outlining the progression). Care must be taken to monitor arousal as each progressive step is labeled. Sometimes it is a good idea to name just a few of the points during one session and save the others for later sessions. This may seem a laborious process, but it is usually a more manageable approach to the trauma for the client. The fact that a traumatic event can be organized can be very reassuring. Moreover, discovering that one piece can be addressed at a time, and that arousal can be contained in between, helps the client to feel safer about dealing with the upsetting material.

SECOND TRAUMA SESSION

During the session, Arlene was able to fill in the missing points from the outline:

3. "Forced to have sex"
4. "Forced to finish"

In tracking her somatic responses, she realized that point #3 was not as upsetting to her as some other aspects of the trauma. The worst part of the rape was her shame about being forced to remove her clothes. The emotion of shame often accompanies trauma, especially trauma that involves intrusion and/or betrayal. Shame can also result from a feeling of failure to protect the self. It is a normal consequence of rape or incest.

We spent the majority of the session working with her feelings of shame. Arlene speculated that perhaps the wealth of shame she was feeling was disproportionate because the rapist was so shameless.

THIRD TRAUMA SESSION

Arlene was ready to establish the safe place and comforting person she would run to as she addressed the circumstances of the rape. She chose a favorite place by the sea, running along the beach and up a sand dune to her best friend, Cheryl. I asked her to draw a map of the route, and then imagine running there from my office. She sat squarely in her chair, feet flat on the floor, and imagined running along the route to and then along the beach, then up the sand dune to be greeted by Cheryl. This brought a flood of emotion as she imagined being received by her friend. Arlene imagined Cheryl saying, "It's over now; you're safe."

As with many clients, Arlene's first run to the safe place, though from a neutral point, was quite moving. As mentioned previously, the fantasy run has two distinct parts, running away from and running to. This practice run emphasized the importance of running to a safe place and being met by someone supportive—something sorely lacking at the time Arlene was raped.

We then began to address elements not on the outline, namely the events following the rape. Often the events following a trauma have as much impact, if not more, than the trauma itself. As noted earlier, I nearly always begin trauma work with the events in the aftermath. This helps to clear up issues that would otherwise make working with the trauma itself too overwhelming.

When Arlene got home after being raped, she telephoned a man she'd felt close to. As she recalled his unsympathetic response, she began to feel angry. She had been devastated when he said, "What did you expect?" After that, she didn't tell anyone about the rape for a long time. I had her imagine running to the beach and her friend Cheryl (whom she had not known at the time). Arlene cried as she realized that Cheryl "would have come over right away. She would have told me that I'd be just fine." For the first time she shed tears of grief over this trauma and over how alone she had been. When her crying subsided, she reported feeling sad but calm.

FOURTH TRAUMA SESSION

Arlene arrived to report that the last session had been very helpful. It was the first time she had mourned what had happened, and it felt good. She now had more of a sense that the rape was in her past, and she was ready to move on and face some of the details.

We continued with the events following the rape. Arlene was haunted by a particular visual image. We used the NLP-inspired technique discussed in Chapter 10, to help her control that image. Arlene found that being able to manipulate so many aspects of the intrusive image helped her to detach from it. She liked doing the manipulations and laughed frequently. She had never known she could control visual images in this way, and it gave her a great feeling of power. She said, "I wish I could have been in that much control *that* night!"

Arlene then began to wonder if she could have stopped the rape from happening. She was scared that she would be vulnerable to being raped again if she didn't figure it out. Banking on the success she'd had manipulating a single image, I suggested that she look at the rape sequence as if it were on a VCR, running the videotape forward or backwards as slow or fast as she wanted. That way she could take an objective "look" at it and identify any places along the way where control or assertiveness might have been possible.

A side note: This can be a tricky process. The client must never feel like the therapist is holding her responsible for getting raped. At the same time, it is imperative that the client strengthen her attention to safety, her assertiveness, and her trust in her own intuition—the necessary tools to help reduce vulnerability to future sexual violence. De Becker's *The Gift of Fear* (1997) addresses this principle in depth. However, this idea cannot be introduced prematurely. To do so would defeat the purpose of gaining control over vulnerability and make the client feel further shamed and victimized. In this case, the timing was good.

Reviewing the trauma on the imagined videotape, Arlene was able to identify three points at the beginning of the rape sequence where she might have been able to stop it had she been more experienced and better resourced. When I asked her to view even earlier scenes, she was able to see four more places, at the very beginning of the date itself, where listening to her instincts might have changed events. Rather than feeling guilty, she felt relieved. She could clearly see that her instincts were intact, though she had ignored them. She was a bit stunned to think that it might have been possible to prevent the rape had she been able to listen to herself. She resolved to take her instincts seriously in the future.

FIFTH TRAUMA SESSION

Arlene reported that since the last session she was finding it easier to set boundaries and say no. She felt that her self-respect had increased and that she had an easier time walking away from situations that she didn't feel comfortable in. She said with astonishment, "I'm not thinking about it; it's just sort of happening." This comment indicated integrated change: She realized that she was behaving differently without planning or effort on her part. Because problems with assertiveness and boundaries were main issues she came to therapy to improve, I saw this change as very positive.

We turned to further addressing the rape. Arlene was still struggling with doubts: Was it really so bad? Am I making this up? Why didn't I see it coming? Believing she was ready to face it, I asked Arlene what the worst part of the trauma was. She replied easily: Being trapped in his apartment. The rapist had turned the double key bolt and kept the key in his pocket, and then he had set the alarm. She had no idea how she could get away, and even if she could, she would trigger the alarm and he would know. We worked with this scene, having her imagine running away from his apartment to her safe place several times.

In her imagined conversations with Cheryl, Arlene realized that she was not responsible for the rape—that the rapist is always responsible for that. Further, she acknowledged that she had been very young and naïve, and that no one had prepared her for the possibility of date rape. She had been taken totally off-guard. She cried as she said, "It wasn't my fault. I had no idea it could happen."

This was a significant turning point. The most important relationship we have in life is to ourself. Trauma often results in a breach of this integral relationship. Those who suffer long-term effects of trauma often believe that because the trauma happened, they must have done something wrong, that they failed to stop it in some way. Such a notion results in an internal schism; a part of the self feels betrayed or let down. In this instance, self-forgiveness—healing the inner rift, reuniting the self—becomes an essential goal of trauma therapy.

SIXTH TRAUMA SESSION

Arlene also identified another "worst" part of the rape: After the act, when she locked herself in the bathroom, she had felt further trapped and didn't know how to get away. Moreover, she had felt dirty and wanted to bathe—to scrub and scrub.

Inspired by TA, I suggested that Arlene imagine taking her current more adult, nurturing self into the scene to escort her younger, more naïve self out of the bathroom and the apartment. Then I had her imagine them running together to the safe place. In the safe place Arlene imagined her nurturing self, along side Cheryl, giving comfort and providing support.

This strategy had two purposes: The first was to aid in healing the relationship to the self. The second was to help Cheryl to separate the past from the present and to see that she *now* was more capable than she was *then*, that she now had additional resources and was more able to care for herself.

Arlene found this variation to be exciting and invigorating. She then began to feel angry—*very* angry—at the rapist for the first time. I had her repeat the scene of escorting herself out several times, helping her to identify the physical sensations of anger. After a couple of tries she spontaneously imagined kicking the rapist in the stomach on the way out. I encouraged her to actually make a kicking motion with her leg, which she said felt good. I further encouraged her to let her angry fantasy evolve. At first she was shy about it, but she soon found it very satisfying.

Revenge fantasies are often part of the healing process, particularly when the trauma involved being harmed by another human. Most clients can take revenge fantasies to whatever extreme is consoling for them without any danger of acting them out or confusing the fantasy with reality. However, with clients who cannot make that distinction, caution must be taken. Revenge fantasies can help to restore and/or build a sense of control and power.

SEVENTH TRAUMA SESSION

Arlene reported that her self-confidence was continuing to improve, and that she was feeling much calmer when remembering the rape. After the last session she had a violent, revengeful dream. She was happy when she woke up; it felt good to express her rage in her dream.

Arlene was now ready to work with the core of the trauma: the actual rape. She had gathered and built up the necessary emotional strength and confidence to face that event. Had we approached this earlier, the chance of retraumatization would have been high.

Arlene admitted that she froze when the rapist locked the door; she felt vulnerable and scared. She believed that the only way to get out again was to give him what he wanted and he said as much. He persisted in his pressure and coercion and she relented out of helplessness and hopelessness. This is a common date rape scenario, especially with young and inexperienced women. When they feel trapped, they believe the only way to get free is to give in. When the man is big, aggressive, and in charge, it is common to fear the consequences of refusal.

I directed Arlene to remember that scene several times, screaming "No!" (aloud) while she imagined fleeing the scene and running to her safe place. I encouraged her to do the same at every instant she had wanted to say no at the time. She cried the first few times upon arrival at the safe place: "I didn't want to have sex! He wouldn't let me go unless I 'finished' him. He didn't give me any choice. I was so scared."

When Arlene originally outlined the rape, I didn't ask her what "forced to finish" meant. It hadn't been a good time to ask her for details; she had been reluctant to name that step in the first place. Now, however, I did ask and she was ready to face how she was forced perform oral sex.

By the fourth run to the safe place Arlene realized consciously what she had known and reacted to unconsciously by freezing and relenting: that it had been impossible for her to get away. He was much bigger and stronger than she was. She was sure she couldn't have fought him off even if she had not frozen. Had she tried, she could have been seriously hurt.

FINAL TRAUMA SESSION

Arlene called mid-week to cancel this session. She said she felt great and believed that she was finished working with the rape and didn't see any more to do. I insisted that she come in for a final session, explaining that I wanted her to go through the entire sequence of events to make sure that there were no missed trigger points, no areas that still evoked hyperarousal. Then, I proposed, she would know for sure she was done with it. She agreed that was a good idea and kept the appointment.

This is an important final step in work with any trauma—repeating the whole story, putting it together, making sense of it as a whole piece of history. It not only helps to root the trauma firmly in the past, but also alerts both therapist and client to any remaining unresolved areas.

I asked Arlene to tell the chronicle of her rape in its entirety—to create a cohesive narrative. This was the first time she had actually recounted the whole incident from start to finish, including all the details. My main concern while listening to her account was to slow her down enough for us both to be vigilant in detecting signs of arousal that might indicate unresolved issues.

There was no cause for worry—Arlene nearly waltzed through the telling. A minor arousal, indicated by slight spaciness, occurred when she remembered being trapped in the apartment. When we focused on that instance she quickly remembered, "But now I know I can run away—unlock the door, slam it on my way out, and run! I feel free." That realization was all that was needed to dissolve the spaciness completely. In the telling, she realized additional points along the way where she might have intervened had she been more savvy. She filed that information for future use.

Arlene told me that since the last two sessions she had felt extreme relief. She reported that she had finally been able to tell her mother what had happened. She no longer felt ashamed. She identified three especially helpful points in the therapy: (1) learning that she could control the intrusive images (2) knowing she could run away, and (3) the revenge fantasies she created.

POSTSCRIPT

Upon contacting Arlene several months after the completion of her therapy, she reported that she felt free of the effects of the rape. She was now able to remember it without hyperarousal. Further, she was more assertive and effective in setting boundaries and limits. Her self-esteem had improved and she no longer suffered bouts of shame and guilt.

CHAPTER EIGHTEEN

Learning from Mistakes and Failure

Even the best therapist fails to help clients at times; it is an unavoidable professional pitfall. As difficult as it is to admit failure, it is even harder to talk about it openly with colleagues. Among some professionals, failure has become a taboo topic. This chapter is written, therefore, with the hope of opening up the subject of therapist failure as a legitimate concern, demystifying it, and making it acceptable to talk about. The use of the word *failure* here does not imply judgement; rather, it is used intentionally in an attempt to decontaminate and desensitize it. It would be good if we could say more easily, "I failed," without fear of external or internal condemnation.

Certainly failure has a down side. We want to avoid it because we want to help our clients. We also want to feel good about the work we do, and admitting failure can threaten our pride and satisfaction in our work. But failure also has an upside when we are able to learn from it.

It makes it possible to hone our craft into something better. Failures can be our greatest teachers.

The introduction to this book included Joseph Wolpe's (1969) admonishment not to blame clients when a therapy fails, but to look at the application of methods for the cause. In addition, we must look at ourselves, including our inexperience, ignorance, and issues of countertransference. Each of these issues is discussed in the context of specific case failures.

SUPERVISION

Most states' licensure requires psychotherapists to have at least 2 years of supervised practice after graduation. Supervision during those 2 years is an extension of classroom education, helping to bridge the gap between what was learned from lectures and books and the application of that knowledge to therapy with clients. Supervision also aids the new psychotherapist in becoming aware of areas of countertransference— both the strengths that may enhance his work and the weaknesses and vulnerabilites that could detract from it.

Following licensure, supervision is still vitally important. It can be useful for helping the most experienced therapist to see her blind spots and avoid hazards. An objective eye is something we all need in this profession. Postlicensure supervision does not need to be as formal as prelicensure supervision: There is no need for evaluation, recommendation, or signing off on hours. Peer supervision groups can be an excellent option.

The need for ongoing supervision increases for those working with traumatized clients. When client histories involve terrifying and horrifying incidents, the risk of countertransference increases. The risk of vicarious traumatization is also omnipresent and vital to prevent

(Rothschild, 2002b). Those of us working with trauma need additional support as well as insightful feedback as we peruse difficult terrain with our clients.

INEXPERIENCE AND IGNORANCE

Usually it is in the early phases of our careers that we do the most regrettable things. Just about every inexperienced therapist makes a big mistake at sometime or another. Most of us would like to forget these early, often embarrassing, *faux pas* and move on. Hopefully we learn from them.

Although inexperience wears off over time, we always remain at risk for ignorance. There is no way any of us can know everything there is to know about trauma treatment: The body of knowledge is far too vast, and it also is constantly evolving. It is certainly a good idea to attempt to keep up. But it is an equally good idea to be comfortable with sometimes just not knowing. Many errors can be made when therapists try to look like they know more than they actually do.

It always astonishes me when a client, student, or someone attending a lecture tells me they liked it when I said "I don't know" in response to a question. What surprises me is that this is such a surprise to them. There are two major things I extract from such feedback. The first is that people appreciate honest ignorance. The other is that they do not get enough of it. The first of the following three cases are examples of how inexperience and ignorance lead to failure.

Lars: Fixed on Technique

Early in my career I was in the habit of concentrating on the therapeutic method I had most recently learned. I was especially dangerous during the weeks following training courses. With blinders on, I would persevere in applying the "therapy *du jour*," neglecting to notice if that was the best strategy for a particular client. Sometimes I was lucky, but other times I was not. All too many clients suffered from my enthusiasm; luckily not all of them became failures.

One failure, though, I remember with particular chagrin. The weekend after an especially exciting training in a new trauma method, I had a new client, Lars, who recently had tragically lost a loved one. During the training we had learned how to work with grief, and I couldn't believe my luck in getting this client. Rather than listening to what he had to say, I pitched the value of the new method for working with grief. Unimaginable to me now, I actually pushed one of the books promoting that method into his hands, encouraging him to read it so he would know how we would work together. He politely returned my book, but, needless to say, he never came back to therapy.

When I discussed this with my supervisor, she first gently reminded me that I needed to learn to listen to my client before I pitched method. She also helped me to realize that this client had not been a good candidate for techniques at all. With his regimented background, anything that smacked of mechanism was abhorrent. He was looking for someone to just talk with him, and I had missed the boat. My eagerness to help and my enthusiasm for my new tool had prevented me from simply meeting my client.

Hanne: Persisting in Uncovering Memories

Over the years several therapists have sought supervision with me because they had clients who were seriously decompensating. This can happen for many reasons, including therapists' attempts to address traumatic memories before the client has sufficient information about the event and/or adequate resources to manage addressing it. The more persistent the therapeutic focus, the worse some clients become. When this occurs, it is advisable to stop the trauma-focused work and prioritize helping the client to stabilize and become functional. Hopefully, at some point the therapist realizes something has gone wrong and seeks supervision.

Most therapists make this error honestly, as there are many schools of thought that promote persisting with work on trauma memories despite decompensation. Though some have modernized their thinking in the last few years, others still adhere to that philosophy. For many years I also believed that was the correct strategy.

Now I know that there is nothing to indicate that addressing trauma memories is the treatment of choice for *all* clients. On the contrary, there is a growing body of literature that indicates that it is *not* always helpful (van der Hart & Steele, 1997; Wolf, Gales, Shane, & Shane, 2000). It pains me to realize that I have sometimes hurt clients by encouraging them to stay focused on trauma when doing that clearly was making them worse.

In the mid-1980s, before I knew very much about trauma therapy or about the risks of persistent memory work, Hanne became my client. She believed her mother had tried to suffocate her when she was a small child. Her physical symptoms, including breathing difficulties when she became stressed as well as periodic nightmares, had led her to that conclusion. She wanted me to help her illuminate those memories and resolve the issues involved.

Using the methods and theories that I had available to me at the time, I tried to help Hanne recall what had happened. We focused on her body sensations, interpreting what must have occurred based on her physical responses and visual images. Over several weeks she had very strong emotional and somatic reactions and began to construct the suspected incident. She became very obsessed with the process, keeping copious notes. She spent countless hours on it in her daily life, unable to talk or think about much else. Gradually, over the next few months, the search for her memories absorbed her whole life. She began to decompensate, having increasing trouble sleeping, eating, and engaging in normal activities. She took a leave from her job and applied for disability. Before that time, I had never had a client become so debilitated by therapy, and I was, needless to say, very concerned.

My then-supervisor was trained in the same school of therapy as I and assumed that the work I was doing with my client was the proper course. He advised me that "sometimes clients need to get worse before they get better, even if they become dysfunctional for a time."

Hanne, however, did not get better. She continued to get worse, even requiring medication to assist in symptom management. At the time, no one, including the prescribing psychiatrist, suggested changing the direction of the therapy. Finally, after nearly a year of this and against my supervisor's advice, I talked Hanne into halting the memory-focused work. I made my case by pointing out her loss of stability and normal functioning, and I urged her to at least take a break from her memory pursuit, suggesting that she could return to it at a future date. I argued that it was more important for her to have a normal life *now* than to know exactly what happened to her as a child.

Hanne ambivalently agreed to try the new tack; she was both relieved and reluctant. She knew she was getting worse and was very frightened for her sanity. But she was also disappointed about abandoning her quest, even temporarily. Over the next few months she gradually stabilized and was able to return to a normal life. Once she was working again, she decided to continue to postpone her memory pursuit, fearful of becoming dysfunctional again.

I learned many things from working with Hanne, but I wish it had not been at the cost of her year of intense suffering. I greatly value the contributions of all of my supervisiors, including the one I was seeing at that time, but they, too, are fallible. When supervisor advice conflicts with my common sense, I now pay more attention. I am also no longer a proponent of continuing in *any* therapeutic direction that results in a worsening of symptoms or a decrease in function.

COUNTERTRANSFERENCE

Countertransference, like transference, can be both positive and negative. It is a good idea to become conscious of countertransference issues, when possible, so that potential problems can be avoided and benefits can be used. When countertransference remains unconscious, it can put a client in jeopardy. It is highly possible, though not proven, that the root of many therapeutic failures can be found in the therapist's unconscious countertransference. This is not to imply that a client has no responsibility or that client resistance and secondary gain do not exist, but rather that how we handle difficulties is largely influenced by countertransference.

Work with trauma is especially demanding. Type IIB clients in particular can be difficult to work with. It is with those clients that issues of transference and countertransference are most important, as well as most volatile.

Conni: Perceived as the Perpetrator

Several times I've found myself in the unfortunate position of being perceived by one of my Type IIB clients as someone who has or could hurt them. They transfer their feelings from a perpetrator who actually did harm them onto me, becoming afraid of me in the process. It is always surprising when I am put in this category because I believe I do so much to prevent it. But try as I might, it can still happen.

There are those who would argue that such transference is inevitable and that it is necessary to the working through of trauma. However, I have never found this to be true with Type IIB clients. On the contrary, I have found it to be destructive. Once the Type IIB client perceives the therapist as someone dangerous, he is no longer an ally. For this type of client, that makes the treatment room a dangerous place to be and therapy a dangerous process.

Why this kind of transference hampers therapy with Type IIB clients but enhances therapy with other clients remains to be examined. But I speculate that it has something to do with the Type IIB client's lower capacity for dual awareness. Other clients usually find it easier to maintain a positive picture of the therapist despite feeling angry or afraid. Once a Type IIB client perceives the therapist as negative or dangerous, however, it is hard to alter that picture.

When this transpires early in the course of therapy, it is fairly easy to make a referral to a colleague if the client's perception cannot be changed. However, when it happens later in therapy, after trust and safety appear to be established, it can be very difficult for both client and therapist.

A few years ago, I encountered this situation with one of my own clients. Through most of the therapy, Conni and I had maintained a fairly good though sometimes stormy relationship. I was an ally walking beside her as she organized her chaotic daily life, and later when she was more stable, examined her very traumatized past. We had periodic conflicts but were able to resolve them. As this client gained in strength, she took greater responsibility for the direction of her therapy, though always with my input and support.

Finally, there was a trauma she wanted to address directly that I did not believe she was ready for, at least in the way she wanted to approach it. We discussed it: I voiced my concerns; she made her case. Eventually I relented. Though I believed it was necessary that it be her choice, there were also countertransference elements involved. I wanted to please her, not to upset her, and so on, but I was not aware of that at the time.

I came to regret my decision. During one of our last sessions Conni proceeded to dive head-first into traumatic memories of an early abuse, insisting that I not stop her at all. She told me she was confident that she could handle it. So, as she requested, I did nothing to interfere. When she got in over her head, becoming hyperaroused and anxious, she continued to insist that I not intercede. She ended up in a panic with a racing heart and cold sweat. She accused me of being the cause of her state, believing I had hurt her. Though she could not pinpoint how, she was certain that something I did had upset her.

We met for several sessions after that, but could not resolve the impasse. For several years I had been one of Conni's major sources of safety, but now she believed I had hurt her. I could find no way to intervene. I discussed the situation in my supervision group, which was helpful for me but not for Conni. Eventually she terminated the therapy, still perceiving me as "dangerous."

In supervision I was able to be open about my feelings. Mostly, I believed I failed Conni by not adequately protecting her; I regretted not holding my ground. My colleagues helped me to see that my counter-transference issue of wanting to please her had conflicted with my good judgement. I had compromised caution for approval.

In previous years, my need to please and be liked by my clients had been a recurring theme in individual supervision. The incident with this client, however, did more to teach me to trust my common sense and hold firm limits—even at the risk of client disapproval—than any supervisor feedback had been able to do. Though I still wish that this therapy had ended differently, I believe I used the lessons to the benefit of many clients since. What I learned from this situation was also instrumental in the evolution of my philosophy of "putting on the brakes."

CHAPTER NINETEEN

Creating Techniques
from Theory

APPLYING COMMON SENSE

In the introduction to this volume, I put forth an argument for a common-sense approach to trauma therapy. I proposed that common sense could be applied to theory to create and adapt interventions suited to individual client situations. Following are two examples of creative interventions gleaned directly from applying common sense to theory. They both feature application of body-oriented techniques: the first for containment; the second to facilitate dual awareness and trauma processing. However, creative and common-sense interventions are by no means limited to body-oriented techniques. The point of this chapter is to inspire readers to reach beyond what they usually do by becoming able to draw upon resources, tools, and knowledge from their own unique backgrounds.

THOMAS: GETTING GLUED

A new client, Thomas, was unstable emotionally and physically. He looked like he was literally coming unglued. He was often dissociated, and when he did feel his body, he experienced it as disconnected, as if none of the parts fit together. Though he recognized this had long been the case, he admitted feeling more unglued in the last 6 months. When he moved he looked disjointed, much like a gangly teenager, although he was well into middle-age. His joints were so unstable that he had suffered several injuries in the last few months: a sprained ankle, dislocated knee, and carpal tunnel syndrome.

Thomas had experienced many traumas in his life. As a result his body was a site of anxiety, pain, and shame, and he was sometimes plagued by intrusions of somatic memories. Dissociating from his body had always represented freedom from suffering. However, being dissociated was also frightening. In the last 8 months he had become interested in yoga, as it made it possible for him to "visit" his body for short bursts and gave him more control.

Thomas and I agreed that the immediate goal of his therapy needed to involve stabilization and increased ability to feel and be in his body. My first impulse was to help him to find his skin, his most physical edge. But that did not turn out to be a good idea. He did not respond well to sensing the container created by his skin. When we tried it, he became anxious and more dissociated. We backed off.

Instead, I suggested that we focus on his "disjointedness." I believed that teaching Thomas to strengthen his joints might help him to "pull himself together," both physically *and* emotionally. But I ran into a problem as I realized that the stretching involved in yoga—one of the few things he really enjoyed—could be contributing to his joint problems. If that was the case, it could also, I feared, be contributing to his emotional decompensation. I needed to find a way to help him stabilize without having to give up the yoga.

Pulling Apart

Sometimes a little education goes a long way, and Thomas was very bright. So I decided to teach him a little anatomy to clarify for him what I believed might be going on. Once he understood, I could then propose a way to solve the problem. He had no knowledge in this area, so I started from scratch. I explained that every skeletal muscle acts on a joint. When a muscle contracts it either bends a joint (flexes), or straightens it (extends). For the flexion or extension to be possible, the opposing muscle must relax; sometimes it is also stretched. For example, to flex the arm the biceps contract to bend it and the triceps on the back of the arm relax; otherwise bending the arm would be impossible. The greater the bend, the more the triceps are stretched. When a bend is extreme, the tissues that hold a joint together underneath the muscles can also be stretched. To illustrate, I had him try bending and straightening his arms, legs, and fingers. We talked about what he discovered and the sensations in his body. I also kept track of Thomas's arousal level, as I did not want him to become overwhelmed. He reacted differently to focusing on his muscles than he did when he focused on his skin. He actually became calmer, which helped to explain why yoga was becoming such a good resource for him.

Once Thomas had grasped these simple concepts, I suggested he try a yoga posture that involved bending a joint while noticing what happened to the muscles involved and to the connective tissues within that joint. He chose a posture that primarily bent the knee, stretching the quadriceps on the front of the thigh. This position required him to balance on his right leg and bend his left. He held his left foot behind him, bring the heel close to his buttocks. As he pulled the heel closer, I asked him to notice what happened to his knee joint.

At this point Thomas became anxious; his respiration accelerated and he paled slightly. When I asked him what was happening, he said that he just realized that continuing to stretch the knee joint could make it more vulnerable for injury, such as the dislocation he had experienced a few months ago. He became scared that he would have to stop doing yoga, which he loved. He nearly panicked.

I asked him to stand on both feet (for greater support) while I reassured him that, on the contrary, my goal was to help him to *better* utilize yoga. When he was sure I meant it, he calmed down. I further explained that I wanted him to be able to identify which positions helped and which could hurt him so that, with the help of his yoga teacher, he could design an optimal program for himself. Seeing it in that light, he became enthusiastic to go on.

Thomas tried other yoga postures with a variety of results. Some of the positions clearly put stress on the joints he was having difficulty with; others did not. In addition, by gauging his level of hyperarousal, he discovered that some of the postures made him feel more anxious and others were calming.

With that information he was ready to fine-tune his yoga practice. He eventually identified which positions were beneficial, injurious, arousing, and calming for him. He continued with some of the postures as originally learned, others he dropped completely, and he and his yoga teacher modified many so he could continue to use them with less emotional and/or physical risk.

Thomas was encouraged by these sessions. He was excited to take control of his body in this way. Never before had he managed such a friendly relationship with it. He liked being able to adapt his yoga program to suit his own individual needs. In addition, the time we spent focusing on his body decreased (but did not eliminate) the incidence of dissociative episodes.

Once Thomas had modified his yoga practice, he was ready for the next step. I wanted to teach him to "gather himself" physically, to pull himself together in his joints.

Pulling Together

From somewhere in my distant past I recalled two exercise systems that I believed might be useful to Thomas. The first, isometric exercise (Obeck, 1966), builds muscle strength without movement. It gained notoriety in the 1960s as being of benefit for long-distance airplane passengers. The second was the Feldenkrais Method (Feldenkrais, 1991), which, among other things, utilizes imagined movement in addition to actual movement on the premise that imagination can be a useful tool for increasing coordination. Some sports-training programs apply the same principle to improve performance.

I thought that a combination of these two approaches might be helpful for Thomas. I found it to be an exciting challenge to tailor an intervention to what I thought Thomas might need.

My intention was to apply these principles from isometric exercise and the Feldenkrais method to help Thomas to slowly, literally, pull his joints together. It was my hypothesis that, if successful, the result could be increased joint *and* emotional stability.

We proceeded slowly, checking any changes in his body sensations and affect along the way. I was aiming for reduced arousal and anxiety.

To start, I had him rest his hand and forearm on the arm of his chair. He was instructed to first concentrate on the joint of his right wrist, imagining the gap between his hand and forearm narrowing. Thomas and I discussed each step and worked together to find the imagery that he could best use to accomplish this. When this type of imagining is done correctly, nerve impulses cause subtle contractions in the associated muscles. With concentration, the contractions can be felt as well as observed.

After trying just one wrist, we stopped so that Thomas could evaluate both somatic and emotional changes. The results were encouraging. He felt a bit calmer overall and symptoms of arousal reduced slightly. We did the other wrist and the result was similarly encouraging.

Thomas could feel the muscles contract slightly. I could also see small movements under his skin—similar to the slight movements of a sleeping dog that runs in its dream. However, whether this task was really accomplishing what I hoped was not yet evident, and it wouldn't be for several weeks. But the fact that he was calming down made it worth continuing.

Now that Thomas had grasped the potential of the exercise, I asked him which joint he would like to try next. He choose his knees because of what we had first identified with the yoga. Following the same procedure, I had him straighten out one leg at a time and imagine the gap between his shin and thigh closing at the knee. Again the results were good: lowered ANS arousal and a greater feeling of calm.

This was very difficult, highly concentrated work. What has been described to this point took a full hour. For homework, Thomas continued with these two exercises for 5–10 minutes two times each day, sticking to it only as long as he continued to get a good response. He knew it was important to monitor his arousal level to make sure the exercises were good for him.

Over the next few sessions, I continued to teach Thomas to pull himself together, one joint at a time. The overall physical result was positive, and his clumsiness and vulnerability to injuries moderated. The increased postural stability generalized to the emotional; he felt more contained and had still fewer incidences of dissociation.

Finally, once a stable foundation was laid, we were able to begin to focus on his traumatic past. The success he had with altering his yoga program combined with the exercises of pulling together worked to gradually make his body a safe place to be. That provided a necessary resource he could use at will to reduce arousal as we traversed the difficult territory of traumatic memories.

SUZANNE: UPDATING THE IMPLICIT THROUGH MOVEMENT

The primary mechanisms that perpetuate PTSD are intrusive images and symptoms of hyperarousal. They are the root cause of flashbacks and the perception that a past trauma is still occurring in the present. Fueled by the ever-active amygdala and unchecked by the adrenaline-suppressed hippocampus, traumatic memory goes haywire.

As noted earlier, memories of emotional states, physical sensations, and visual and auditory images are all stored in the implicit memory system. They return unbidden, automatically set in motion, the conditioned response of conditioned stimuli. Integration is impossible because the time and space context usually supplied by the hippocampus is missing.

For trauma to be resolved, the memory of it must be assigned to its rightful place in the past. Sometimes physical movement facilitates this process, particularly when trauma involved restriction or paralysis of any kind—by circumstances (such as hiding), at the hands of another (restraint), or even the freeze response itself. When the physical experience is recalled, it can be an excellent opportunity to update the implicit memory system. Movement has the potential to send the nonverbal message that the trauma is in the past and something is different *now*.

Forty-eight-year-old Suzanne remembered her childhood bout with polio well. Though she had made a full recovery and had full use of her arms and legs, there were scars. We worked on many aspects of her illness—fear of dying, fear of pain, etc.—using several methods, EMDR being the most effective. The worst part for Suzanne, however, was feeling abandoned during her month-long confinement in an iron lung. Recalling the sense of loneliness and restriction was overwhelming. We approached these core issues carefully from several angles and resolved much of it. But a nagging anxiety still remained. The central negative cognition associated with her ordeal persisted: "I can't move on my own behalf." I decided we needed to try something different to help her past this block.

It occurred to me that, on some level, Suzanne still believed that she could not move, despite the everyday evidence that she could. If that weren't true, she would not be identifying with the negative cognition that perpetuated that belief. She was living a dichotomy: In her daily life she constantly moved, but she could not use this fact to relieve her continuing distressed state. In therapy, she almost never moved, especially when focusing on her traumatic past. In addition, so far, no type or amount of work—either with EMDR or dual awareness—had changed her perception of being unable to move. I needed to find a way to help her realize on all levels that her situation was different *now*. Spontaneously I came up with an idea that was so simple I could not believe I had not tried it before.

I proposed that the next time Suzanne became immobile while processing with EMDR, we would make one slight alteration: I wanted her to use physical walking for the bilateral stimulation. We constructed the usual protocol, including her persistent negative cognition. When it was time for eye movements, I had her get up and walk instead. I instructed her to focus on both the shift between right and left, and also on the movement itself. We were both pleased to find this had a multifold effect. First, getting up and walking wrenched Suzanne out of the feeling of paralysis and restriction. Second, it provided the necessary bilateral stimulation for the EMDR processing. Third, on a somatic level it communicated a new message to both her body and mind—"I can move." Fourth, it updated her implicit memory system—"I can move *now*."

Amazingly, the minor alteration worked well. The therapeutic roadblock was removed; the negative cognition of "I can't move on my own behalf" changed to a positive cognition of "I can move whenever I want." This made processing the remaining issues from her illness smooth, as her implicit memory of restriction had been updated.

This same idea can be applied with other therapy methods. When freezing or restriction is an issue, even simply asking a client to get up, change position, or actively move a leg or an arm while narrating or processing a traumatic incident can be enough to send the message that things are different *now*.

Summing Up

Just as no two people are alike, no two trauma clients are alike. Each one needs to be treated with regard for her own particular situation and her own special needs.

Through the cases in this volume I have endeavoured to illuminate the usefulness of having many psychotherapy and trauma therapy tools at hand for the treatment of trauma and PTSD. If I have been successful, you now should have an idea of how you might adapt the methods and models that you are, yourself, trained in for use with your own traumatized clients. Hopefully, you have also been inspired to learn more about other methods, through reading, taking courses, or signing up for a training program.

I am fully convinced that if you exercise and increase your ability to use your own common sense, adapting methods and models to the needs of your individual clients will become second nature.

Many people ask about and speculate on what the future holds for trauma therapy. Many hope that their particular model or method will be *the* treatment of choice for all clients. As you might have guessed by now, no matter what that model could be, I hope that there will never be just *one* preferred treatment of choice. The future of trauma treatment must include a wide variety of trauma methods. Each therapist needs to be trained in several so that there is a smorgasbord of interventions available to therapists and their clients.

I also believe that we will soon have better tools for distinguishing which clients are candidates for resolving their trauma memories and which would best benefit from focus on stabilization of their daily life.

In conclusion, I hope that the future of trauma therapy—all psychotherapy for that matter—includes a liberal use of common sense in the choice and application of treatment methods with all clients.

Further Information and Reading on Therapy Models

B elow are suggestions of books and websites on the therapy models discussed in this volume. Where no definitive website was available, none is given. However, updated information and numerous additional websites can be found through inquires on any of the Internet's biggest search engines: yahoo.com, google.com, etc. Contact information for organizations is not included here because it can quickly become outdated.

General Information on Trauma:

International Society for Traumatic Stress Studies website: *www.istss.org*

National Center for PTSD website: *www.ncptsd.org*

David Baldwin's Trauma Pages website: *www.trauma-pages.com*

Applications of Attachment Theory

Schore, A. (1994). *Affect regulation and the origin of the self*. Hillsdale, NJ: Lawrence Erlbaum Associates.

Siegel, D. J. (1999). *The developing mind*. New York: Guilford.

Bodynamic Running Technique

Rothschild, B. (1996/7). An annotated trauma case history: Somatic trauma therapy, part I. *Somatics, 11*(1), 48–53.

Rothschild, B. (1997). An annotated trauma case history: Somatic trauma therapy, part II. *Somatics, 11*(2), 44–49.

Bodynamic website (in English): www.bodynamicusa.com

Body Psychotherapy

United States Association for Body Psychotherapy website: www.usabp.org

European Association for Body Psychotherapy website: www.eabp.org

Cognitive Behavioral Therapy

Linehan, M. (1993). *Cognitive-behavioral treatment of borderline personality disorder*. New York: Guilford.

Wolpe, J. (1969). *The practice of behavior therapy*. London: Pergamon.

Center for the Treatment and Study of Anxiety website: www.med.upenn.edu/ctsa

Eye Movement Desensitization and Reprocessing (EMDR)

Shapiro, F. (1995). *Eye movement desensitization and reprocessing: Basic principles, protocols, and procedures*. New York: Guilford.

EMDR International Association website: www.emdria.org

Gestalt Therapy

Polster, E., & Polster, M. (1974). *Gestalt therapy integrated*. New York: Random House.

International Gestalt Therapy Association website: www.gestalt.org

Levine's SIBAM Model

Levine, P. (1992). *The body as healer: Transforming trauma and anxiety*. Lyons, CO: Author.

Somatic Experiencing website: www.traumahealing.com

Neuro-Linguistic Programming (NLP)

Bandler, R., & Grinder, J. (1975). *The structure of magic*. Palo Alto, CA: Science and Behavior Books.

Psychodynamic Psychotherapy

Horowitz, M. J. (1988). *Introduction to psychodynamics: A new synthesis*. New York: Basic Books.

Psychopharmacology as an Adjunct to Trauma Therapy

Preston, J. D. (2002). *Handbook of clinical psychopharmacology for therapists, Third edition*. Oakland, CA: New Harbinger.

Somatic Trauma Therapy

Rothschild, B. (2000). *The body remembers: The psychophysiology of trauma and trauma treatment*. New York: Norton.

Somatic Trauma Therapy website: www.trauma.cc

Transactional Analysis

Berne, E. (1961). *Transactional analysis in psychotherapy*. New York: Grove.

Goulding, M. M., & Goulding, R. L. (1979). *Changing lives through redecision therapy*. New York: Bruner/Mazel. (Rev. ed., Grove, 1997.)

International Transactional Analysis Association website: www.itta-net.org

References

American Psychiatric Association. (1980). *Diagnostic and statistical manual of mental disorders* (3rd ed.). Washington DC: Author.

American Psychiatric Association. (1994). *Diagnostic and statistical manual of mental disorders* (4th ed.). Washington DC: Author.

Andreas, A., & Andreas, T. (1987). *Change your mind and keep the change: Advanced NLP submodalities interventions*. Moab, UT: Real People Press.

Bandler, R. (1985). *Using your brain—for a change*. Moab, UT: Real People Press.

Bandler, R., & Grinder, J. (1975). *The structure of magic*. Palo Alto, CA: Science and Behavior Books.

Berne, E. (1961). *Transactional analysis in psychotherapy*. New York: Grove.

Bodynamic Institute. (1988–1992). Training program. Copenhagen, Denmark.

Bremner, J. D., Southwick, S., Brett, E., Fontana, A., Rosenheck, R., & Charney, D. S. (1992). Dissociation and posttraumatic stress disorder in Vietnam combat veterans. *American Journal of Psychiatry, 149,* 328–332.

Carlson, E. B. (1996). Psychometric review of dissociative experiences scale (DES). In B. H. Stamm (Ed.), *Measurement of stress trauma and adaptation* (pp. 152–157). Lutherville, MD: Sidran Press.

Classen, C., Koopman, C., & Spiegel, D. (1993). Trauma and dissociation. *Bulletin of the Menninger Clinic, 57*(2), 178–194.

de Becker, G. (1997). *The gift of fear*. New York: Little, Brown.

de Boer-van der Kolk, B. (1998, November). *Integrating body-oriented techniques in a conventional psychodynamically oriented clinical practice*. Presentation at the annual meeting of the International Society for Traumatic Stress Studies. Washington, D.C.

Feldenkrais, M. (1991). *Awareness through movement: Health exercises for personal growth*. San Francisco: Harper.

Foa, E. B., Keane, T. M., & Friedman, M. J. (Eds.). (2000). *Effective treatments for PTSD*. New York: Guilford.

Freud, S. (1953). On Psychotherapy. In J. Strachey (Ed. and Trans.), *The standard edition of the complete psychological works of sigmund freud* (Vol. 7, pp. 257–268). London: Hogarth Press. (Original work published 1905)

Gallup, G. G., & Maser, J. D. (1977). Tonic immobility: Evolutionary underpinnings of human catalepsy and catatonia. In M. E. P. Seligman & J. D. Masser (Eds.), *Psychopathology: Experimental models*. San Francisco: W. H. Freeman.

Gerardin, E., Sirigu, A., Lehericy, S., Poline, J. B., Gaymard, B., Marsault, C., Agid, Y., & Le Bihan, D. (2000). Partially overlapping neural networks for real and imagined hand movements. *Cerebral Cortex, 10*(11), 1093–1104.

Goulding, M. M., & Goulding, R. L. (1979). *Changing lives through redecision therapy*. New York: Bruner/Mazel. (Rev. ed., Grove, 1997.)

Herman, J. L. (1992). *Trauma and recovery*. New York: Basic.

Jeannerod, M. (1995). Mental imagery in the motor context. *Neuropsychologia, 33*(11), 1419–1432.

Jørgensen, S. (1992). Bodynamic analytic work with shock/post-traumatic stress. *Energy and Character, 23*(2), 30–46.

Jørgensen, S. (Ed.). (1993). *Forløsning af choktraumer*. Copenhagen: Kreatik.

Levine, P. (1992). *The body as healer: Transforming trauma and anxiety*. Lyons, CO: Author.

Levine, P. (1997). *Waking the tiger*. Berkeley, CA: North Atlantic Books.

McGoldrick, M., Gerson, R., & Shellenberger, S. (1999). *Genograms: Assessment and interventions* (2nd ed.). New York: Norton.

Nadel, L., & Jacobs, W. J. (1996). The role of the hippocampus in PTSD, panic, and phobia. In N. Kato (Ed.), *Hippocampus: Functions and clinical relevance* (pp. 455–463). Amsterdam: Elsevier.

Nijenhuis, E. R., Spinhoven, P., van Dyck, R., van der Hart, O., & Vanderlinden, J. (1996). The development and psychometric characteristics of the Somatoform Dissociation Questionnaire (SDQ-20). *Journal of Nerve and Mental Disease, 184*(11), 688–694.

Obeck, V. (1966). *Isometrics: The static way to physical fitness*. New York: Stravon Educational Press.

Perls, F. (1942). *Ego, hunger and aggression*. Durban, South Africa: Knox Publishing.

Phillips, C. & Frederick, C. (1995). *Healing the divided self: Clinical and Ericksonian hypnotherapy for post-traumatic and dissociative conditions*. New York: Norton.

Post, R. M., Weiss, S. R., Li, H., Smith, M. A., Zhang, L. X., Xing, G., Osuch, E. A., & McCann, U. D. (1998). Neural plasticity and emotional memory. *Development and psychopathology, 10*(4), 829–855.

Rothschild, B. (1996/1997). An annotated trauma case history: Somatic trauma therapy, part I. *Somatics, 11*(1), 48–53.

Rothschild, B. (1997). An annotated trauma case history: Somatic trauma therapy, part II. *Somatics, 11*(2), 44–49.

Rothschild, B. (2000). *The body remembers: The psychophysiology of trauma and trauma treatment.* New York: Norton.

Rothschild, B. (2002a). Bodypsychotherapy without touch: Applications for trauma therapy. In T. Staunton (Ed.), *Body psychotherapy* (pp. 101–115). East Sussex, UK: Bruner-Routledge.

Rothschild, B. (2002b, July/August). Case studies: The dangers of empathy. *Psychotherapy Networker, 26*(4), 61–69.

Schore, A. (1994). *Affect regulation and the origin of the self.* Hillsdale, NJ: Erlbaum.

Selye, H. (1956). *The stress of life.* New York: McGraw-Hill.

Shapiro, F. (1995). *Eye movement desensitization and reprocessing: Basic principles, protocols, and procedures.* New York: Guilford.

Siegel, D. J. (1999). *The developing mind.* New York: Guilford.

Steele, A. (2001, October). *An introduction to imaginal nurturing with EMDR in the treatment of adult clients with insecure attachment.* Presentation at the annual general meeting of the EMDR Association of Canada. Vancouver, BC.

Terr, L. (1994). *Unchained memories.* New York: Basic.

van der Hart, O., & Steele, K. (1997). Relieving or reliving childhood trauma? A commentary on Miltenburg and Singer. *Theory and Psychology, 9*(4), 533–540.

van der Kolk, B. A. (1994). The body keeps the score. *Harvard Review of Psychiatry, 1,* 253–265.

Watkins, H. (1993). Ego-state therapy: An overview. *American Journal of Clinical Hypnosis, 35*(4), 232–240.

Weiss, D. (1996). Psychometric review of the Impact of Events Scale—Revised. In B. H. Stamm (Ed.). *Measurement of stress trauma and adaptation* (pp. 186–188). Lutherville, MD: Sidran Press.

Westen, D., & Morrison, K. (2001). A multidimensional meta-analysis of treatments for depression, panic, and generalized anxiety disorder: An empirical examination of the status of empirically supported therapies. *Journal of Consulting and Clinical Psychology, 69*(6), 875–899.

Wolf, N. S., Gales, M., Shane, E., & Shane, M. (2000). Mirror neurons, procedural learning, and the positive new experience: A developmental systems self psychology approach. *Journal of the American Academy of Psychoanalysis, 28*(3), 409–430.

Wolpe, J. (1969). *The practice of behavior therapy*. London: Pergamon Press.

Wolpe, J. (1958). *Psychotherapy by reciprocal inhibition*. Stanford, CA: Stanford University Press.

Index